Jerome A. Anderson

Reincarnation

A Study of the Human Soul in its Relation to Re-Birth, Evolution, etc.

Jerome A. Anderson

Reincarnation
A Study of the Human Soul in its Relation to Re-Birth, Evolution, etc.

ISBN/EAN: 9783337187569

Printed in Europe, USA, Canada, Australia, Japan

Cover: Foto ©Lupo / pixelio.de

More available books at **www.hansebooks.com**

Jerome A. Anderson M.D. F.T.S.

REINCARNATION.

~ A ~

Study of the Human Soul

In its Relation to Re-Birth,
Evolution, Post-Mortem States, the
Compound Nature of Man, Hypnotism, Etc.

BY

JEROME A. ANDERSON, M. D., F. T. S.

"It is decisive of the question whether the Soul exists if among the activities and emotional states of our being there are to be found such as do not belong to our bodies."—ARISTOTLE.

THE LOTUS PUBLISHING COMPANY,

1504 Market Street, San Francisco, Cal.

MAY 8, 1893.

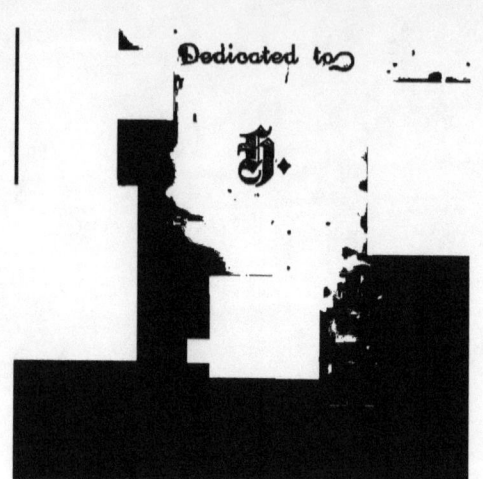

Dedicated to

PREFACE.

THESE pages are intended to present, in as concise a form as possible, an outline of certain phenomena in nature, together with logical and philosophical deductions therefrom, which go to prove, first, the existence of a soul, and, second, the repeated incarnation of this soul in physical bodies. No phenomena will be considered except such as have been fully verified and accepted as a portion of the *armamentarium* of modern science. That there are vast classes of genuine phenomena not acknowledged as genuine by science is well known; and, although fully entitled to an appeal to these in support of our position, it has been thought best to pass them by, and to meet modern scientific agnosticism entirely upon the territory of its own facts. It is believed that by thus "carrying the war into Egypt" more good may be accomplished in directing attention towards the higher spiritual aspects of these phenomena than if the argument were advanced into disputed domains. This completely bars access to an immense mass of so-called spiritualistic phenomena which, while very far from establishing the fact of spirit communication in the manner claimed by spiritualists, are still of great importance as illustrating many of the lower psychic faculties of man, and his essential independence of his body in their production. The numerous marvels of many countries, and especially of India, have also been omitted; for they, although partly accepted by scientists, who fancy they find in "glamour" and "collective hallucination" an explanation, are still an unclassified residuum, whose scientific explanation itself needs to be explained even more than the phenomena for which it attempts to account. In short, the purpose of this book is to establish the fact of the existence and repeated rebirth of the soul by an appeal to logic and reason alone, based upon phenomena of such universal and every-day experience that all who choose may verify each successive step taken, or phenomenon to which reference is had.

The writer was bitterly antagonized by the idea of reincarnation when he first became familiar with it in Theosophic literature ; but, after careful and earnest attempts to arrive at a philosophic or scientific hypothesis in harmony with natural phenomena which would render this view unnecessary, he was compelled by sheer force of facts and logic to accept it. The trains of reasoning followed, and the phenomena appealed to are outlined in these pages. They are issued in the hope of aiding others who may have become, as the writer had, biased toward materialistic views by a one-sided "scientific" education, to recognize this grand truth. The attention of inquirers is also called to the scholarly work of the late E. D. Walker, and to the occult, intuitional, and philosophic Manual by Mrs. Annie Besant, both being upon the same subject—Reincarnation.

J. A. A.

CONTENTS.

INTRODUCTION.

HAPTER I.

CHAPTER II.

CHAPTER III.

CHAPTER IV.

CHAPTER V.

CHAPTER VI.

CHAPTER VII.

CHAPTER VIII.

CHAPTER IX.

CHAPTER X.

CHAPTER XI.

CHAPTER XII.

CHAPTER XIII.

CHAPTER XIV.

APPENDIX.

INTRODUCTION.

THE NATURE AND ORIGIN OF THE SOUL.

THE term "Soul" may be defined as a vehicle for consciousness. The latter, as one of the triple aspects of
the Unknowable or Absolute, must be regarded as infinite.
Anything which, by limiting this infinity, enables consciousness to manifest upon finite and knowable planes is
therefore classed as Soul. The Universal Soul, under this
definition, would be the vehicle for Universal—not Absolute—Consciousness; the human soul, the vehicle for the
finite manifestation of that limitation of the Infinite which
we recognize as human, or self-consciousness.

The material aspect of the Unknowable seems to be
the means by which Infinite Consciousness is enabled to
manifest finitely. Hence, all Soul has its ultimate essence
in this material or Substance-root of the Unknowable, and
is of a material nature. But the three Aspect-Roots—
the third being Motion or Force—are eternally associated,
so that one must not fall into the error of taking a too
materialistic view of Soul. If it is the material vehicle of
consciousness in one aspect, it is in another—by virtue of
its being incapable of dissociation from this—consciousness
itself. It is only because of philosophic necessities and of
certain phenomena of consciousness upon the material
plane that Soul is thus more intimately associated with the
Substance-Aspect of the Unknowable Rootless Root than
with the Conscious-Aspect.

A human soul, then, is a center of consciousness having

its origin in Infinite Consciousness, and limited and
brought into self-conscious relations with itself and the
Universe by a material vehicle. In its inmost essence,
this material vehicle is derived from the indestructible
Substance-Aspect of the Unknowable; substance of so refined and ethereal a nature as to utterly transcend all
those properties and qualities with which we ordinarily associate matter, and which, because of this and because it
is incapable of weight, measurement or even comparison
with the matter of this plane, has led to the formulating
of the absurdly unscientific and unphilosophic materialistic
hypotheses and philosophies of to-day. Instead of following, by correspondence and analogy, the retreat of
matter into those realms which for us are at present subjective, both modern science and so-called materialistic
philosophy have failed to recognize the philosophic necessity for that Unity which must underlie every aspect of
nature, and have in consequence utterly failed to bridge
the illusionary chasm which seems to divide spirit—or
consciousness—from matter. It is, of course, impossible
to carry molecular physics grossly and bodily over into
conscious realms; but it is quite possible, and the only
philosophic procedure, to carry the molecular laws of the
conservation of force and the correlation of energy over
into the realms of (comparatively) pure consciousness.
By so doing, we at once secure a firm and stable foundation for our philosophic superstructure. There is no
longer a necessity for "scientific" laws and hypotheses for
one kingdom of nature, and quite a different and con-
flicting code for another, as is the case with modern scientific attempts to deal with mind and matter as though
they were totally separate and distinct elements in the

Universe. The same lack of an unifying base is also painfully apparent in dealing with purely physical sciences; as, for example, in the disagreements of geologic and astronomic calculations of the age of the earth.

It follows from the above that "Soul" must be a generic term, and "Souls" capable of infinite gradation and classification. From the *anima mundi*, the " Over-Soul" of Emerson, down to the unifying center of consciousness which makes possible the molecular combination forming the structure of the humblest *amœba*—aye, down to that diffuse attraction which combines even inorganic nature into form—the term "Soul" applies. For the material Universe, from our puerile, finite point of view at least, would seem to be a vast evolutionary laboratory constructed in Space and Time, into which enters pure Spirit, or Consciousness, and which, forever disappearing as such, eternally reappears in endless intelligent variations and transmutations of form. Form is but the result of Infinite Consciousness seeking finite expression in matter. Every tree is a materialized or externalized idea; every flower, a sculptured poem; every appearance of form, a passing from Infinite Ideation into finite expression through finite limitation: and all this under law so absolute, so inviolable, that a single exception to or escape from its universal domain is unthinkable. This law, the one stable bond which unites the knowable to the Unknowable, the finite to the Infinite, is that of Cause and Effect; the Karma of Eastern philosophy and modern Theosophy. Its objective arc appears upon this plane under the guise of Evolution; its subjective arc, when not entirely ignored, is known as Involution. An involution of spirit, or consciousness, equals an evolution of matter into form.

"Soul," therefore, in the abstract, stands for and is the Substance-Aspect of the Unknowable, by means of which both involution and evolution of the Conscious-Aspect, or "Spirit," is accomplished.

Yet, throughout this work, by the term "human soul" is meant a self-conscious center of Consciousness—not a center of Substance. The latter limits, defines and makes possible the existence of this individualized center; but while an absolutely necessary element, this necessity would seem somewhat mechanical. The Conscious-Aspect, the "I," the Unit of Consciousness, by which alone the finite universe may be measured and known, is the supreme essential. If it be, apparently, confused with its relatively lower material vehicle by speaking of it as the human soul, it is because of the poverty of the English language in accurate metaphysical terms, and also because it can not, even in thought, be entirely dissociated from this vehicle. That by the human soul is really understood a center of self-consciousness, and not its substance base, will become plainly apparent when, in the course of this study, we shall find this center using "souls," or vehicles, composed of varying differentiations of Substance, accordingly as it functions upon objective or—to us—subjective planes.

REINCARNATION.

A STUDY OF THE SOUL.

CHAPTER I.

THE PHYSIOLOGICAL EVIDENCE OF THE EXISTENCE OF THE SOUL.

A STUDY of the Soul, or of those phenomena of consciousness usually classed under this head, must logically be prefaced by proof that a "soul" really exists. Some doubt arises as to whether this can be best accomplished by an examination of those general evolutionary processes which lead up to the human soul as a necessary sequence, or whether the phenomena of human consciousness itself shall be first considered. As appeal will be taken to both classes of phenomena, it has been thought best to begin with the latter method, leaving the broader and more philosophic generalizations of evolution to follow. The evidence of a soul, then, will be sought first in Human Physiology.

Without cumbering the argument with histological, anatomical, or even physiological details, to be found in the numerous text-books upon these subjects, let it suffice to state generally that these and allied sciences prove that the human body is a mechanism constructed and controlled from within, without, by a central energy called variously "mind," "soul," "spirit," or "Ego," according to the inclination or bias of the writer. The existence of this central energy is disputed by no one; the issue being as to the relation it sustains to the body. Broadly defined, Materialism declares the mind or soul to be the product of the molecular activities going on within the brain; or, if not a direct product, at least a concomitant of these. Under this view, it must necessarily cease to exist when the brain molecules cease their activities. To account for the appearance of a conscious factor as an outcome of purely mechanical motion among molecules, it declares this to be a "property" of matter, capable of being exhibited under certain conditions similarly as electricity may be made to manifest its presence under proper excitation. Spiritualism takes directly the opposite view. It declares that, while it is true that molecular activities are the counterparts of conscious experience, upon this plane, the relation of effect is entirely upon the material side; that the mind or soul is causal, and quite superior to and independent of the body, except as this is a mechanism of sense organs constructed and synthesized by it, in order to relate its higher consciousness to material planes. There can thus be no compromise; one or the other theory errs.

A little examination makes it evident that all thought, emotion, willing or feeling arise from and in the inner recesses of our being, and are then reflected outwards in speech or action, or remain as unexpressed, subjective ideas or feelings. It is quite true that this inner arousing is apparently due primarily to external stimuli alone, and that all through life external impressions transmuted into sensations form a much larger basis for even the highest intellectual life than would be suspected except upon a searching analysis. But *ex nihilo nihil fit;* and if there were not present in the body a potential center of conciousnèss capable of being aroused, external stimuli might knock for eternal ages at the door of life without awakening a conscious response.

Here, at the first step, then, the battle for the existence of the soul begins. For when physiologists or psychologists say, though ever so glibly and confidently, that an external stimulus has been converted through nervous "shock" into a "sense" impression, they are assuming to explain a process of which they have absolutely no knowledge, and which no microscope nor culture chamber has ever demonstrated, nor can ever hope to demonstrate. For, "if by nervous shock be meant a psychical event, the break between such shock and the nerve commotion which is its antecedent is absolutely impassible. No physical energy, under the general laws of its conservation and correlation, can pass this break."* Nor no lightly leaping across a chasm proves its non-existence. In sound, for example, an entirely mechanical and physical shock has been transmuted into terms of consciousness utterly unlike its cause. Until it can be shown both how and why mechanical motion becomes sensation, two factors must be assumed. These are the receiver and transmitter of the nervous shock or commotion, and the inner observer of this commotion, as it records itself in molecular agitation or changes within the brain.

It will be cheerfully admitted that this inner observer is

---

*Ladd's Physiological Psychology, p. 628, to which magnificent work I am more indebted in the preparation of this chapter than any quotation marks can adequately indicate.

quite dependent upon the physical apparatus for sensation upon and communication with the material plane, but this dependence in no way argues its non-existence as an entity, or the non-possibility of its possessing much higher powers upon its own spiritual plane than its sense organs enable it to display upon this. As has been beautifully pointed out by Prof. Ladd:

"Beings do not lose their reality, or characteristic nature, or value in the universe of Being, because they are causally connected with other beings. On the contary, none but real beings can thus be connected with each other; none but real beings can act and be acted upon. The so-called causal connection is no bondage of such nature as to destroy the nature of the beings which act under it. Only beings that have natures of their own can be causally connected. In other words, all that appears to us as a causal relation between the objects of our experience is, ultimately considered, due to no material spur or whip which urges, or band that represses, as though one kind of real being could thus dominate and subdue another. No atom acts without being acted on; what it does depends both upon what it is and also upon how it stands related to other atoms."*

The break between physical motion and conscious sensation, if there really be one, is between the sentient atom and the physical molecule. And Prof. Ladd is therefore quite correct in insisting that:

"No relation exists between these two kinds of beings [soul and body] which can be represented as an interchange of physical energy, under the law of the conservation and correlation of such energy. This fact, however, affords no objection to our recognizing a true causal connection between the two, unless we are ready to insist upon the monstrous claim that modern physical science is entitled to affirm the impossibility of any interaction (or conditional action) taking place in the universe otherwise than between material atoms under the aforesaid law."†

---

*Loc. Cit., p. 661.   †Loc. Cit., p. 663 et seq.

Yet the soul is not utterly unrelated to the body by the actual transmission of energy; for were this the case a physical response to the will would be impossible. There is a transmission of energy from the soul to the body, actual and real, but it does not consist in the ebbing and flowing of physical force The soul may be said to use modes of the "inter-etheric force" of Keeley, for its material base is composed necessarily of these inner and more potent states of matter. These forces the soul liberates in willing, which latter results in motion upon its own plane; and this, while not interchanging, is the cause of a corresponding molecular motion on the plane below. It is thus true that each cycle of energy is unrelated in the way of the conservation or correlation of the energy of one plane upon that of the other; for each completes its cycle in its own proper field of action, and no mode of force belonging to one plane passes over from that to another. But each can none the less act upon the other; and, in the case of the soul, the terrible inter-etheric nature of the energy used may be seen in instances of the sudden death of the body from fright, anger or strong emotion. Physical force and soul, or will-force, touch each other's boundaries, but the very rebound keeps each acting in its own proper domain. Yet this touch is actual, and sets up motion on the other plane; though, as correctly pointed out by Prof. Ladd, nothing physical passes from the one to the other. Nor does anything physical pass when one moving billiard ball strikes another, yet the latter is none the less set in motion. In the same manner there is no plane of the manifested cosmos utterly unrelated to others. Effects may pass though causes do not.

The human nervous system is plainly a mechanism to relate entities thus acting upon different planes and using dissimilar modes of force. It has its end-organs to receive impacts from without, or those from the material world; its system of nerve-wires to conduct—not the shocks, but certain effects of these entirely unlike them in essence— to the brain and minor ganglia; and, lastly, these ganglionic collections of gray matter, to receive and to send out counter-shocks or commotions to other appropriate end-organs, which cause motion in response to such stimuli. Yet in this, which seems so entirely mechanical, there has entered a factor which has hopelessly removed it from the domain of material physics, and which demonstrates that by means of the highly complex nervous organism the body has been related to the plane of spirit, or consciousness. Motion has been translated into terms of sensation, a thing unthinkable except as the act of a conscious entity. Motion can not become sensation; it can only be recognized as motion by a conscious entity, and conscious inferences or information deduced therefrom. A billiard ball may be made to strike another, and this still another; but no synthesizing power arises out of the original impact or resulting motion. Nor could such power arise though force enough were used to keep the whole set caroming among each other for ages. Logic and reason absolutely require the presence of the conscious factor to take note of the molecular commotion caused by the physical impact, and to originate upon its part new and appropriate molecular agitations in response, in the manner indicated.

There must be, then, a conscious entity moving both billiard balls and brain molecules, else neither could ever synthesize themselves into orderly sequences. That there are certain complex reflex responses continually taking place, which are even absolutely necessary to our existence, without rising to the plane of our brain or mind consciousness, does not weaken, but rather strengthens, the argument for such an entity. For the greater the complexity of the mechanism, the greater the necessity for an intelligent, synthesizing center of consciousness to control this complexity. And, as evolution shows, these minor centers of activity are lower entities, in a universe which is but embodied consciousness of some degree, working their way upward in the scale of becoming, and aided very materially by this association with a superior directing and controlling energy.

The psychical experiences arising from physical energy acting upon the periphery of the body are too unlike that energy to be related directly thereto. There are many physiological processes necessary before the energy rises above the threshold of consciousness as a psychical experience. What these are physiology can not explain, and psychology is equally helpless. At the physical side they may be first simply dynamic, and then complex or chemical; at the psychic threshold, they must be the perceptions of a conscious, cognizing entity. In man alone this entity is self-conscious, but an entity of some degree is none the less present in every form of organic life as its synthesizer and organizer. That even in man the relation between this inner cognizer and the form through which it acts is intimate and mutually dependent, goes without saying. The immediate agent in this intimacy is undoubtedly the mechanism of the nervous system, the duty of which is to concatenate or synthesize the sense impressions arising out of the innumerable physical impacts upon the periphery of the body. But a mechanism requires a mechanic, and this is plainly the inner soul. There can be no equality between a mere mechanism, as such, and the intelligence which directs it. In the case of man, too, the mechanism does not express the entire powers of its inner mover, which of itself quite disproves the materialistic theory, however much we might otherwise be inclined to accept it. There is positively no physical equivalent possible for any of the higher faculties. What particular motion among the molecules of the brain can .be postulated as the physical equivalent and causal antecedent of our conceptions of justice, of truth, of moral obligation? The feeblest mind revolts against such a crass conception of its native powers. Perception and sensation may be conceived of as arising out of physical correlates, but no such correlate can be conceived of the being who moves about, as it were, among these, selecting this one and rejecting that. The physical brain is limited to motion only; it can not choose its own mode of motion even.

Of these powers, which even the wildest materialism can not connect with any physical process, the unity of consciousness is perhaps the most convincing proof of the existence of a soul. Unity is unique in consciousness; it is undefinable, unapproachable; yet none the less it IS; and every act, thought, emotion, willing or feeling is, consciously or unconsciously, built upon and referred to this underlying unit, the "I am I." All the myriad states of consciousness are recognized by this "I" as its own. The states, indeed, may result from external causes in nature, or internal, within the organism; but the "I," the unit of consciousness, the synthesizer of them all, has no such relation. It is, in truth, a reflection of that incomprehensible

Unity which is One and yet All, at the dawn of a manvantara. No number of successive states of consciousness can constitute the unity which synthesizes and connects them all. The string of pearls must have a real string, or they are but individual gems, not a sequence of them. Nor can any conceivable number of molecules constitute unity, for upon their own plane each is a unit, and no mere combination of them can produce self-conscious unity upon a higher. They can be synthesized by unity from above into a complex system upon their own plane, but even in this relation they are units grouped, not unity.

Again, the mind is a unit, or it could not perceive itself at all. If it were composed of a complexity of varying states it would exist only as such variety, and no one state would have any real hold upon or memory of those past, or anticipation of those to come. We can not conceive, much less perceive, any quality in nature which we do not possess. It would be so foreign, so utterly unrelated to our consciousness that we might owe our very being to it without being aware of its existence. Unity can alone recognize unity—can alone construct unit things out of the objects in nature. We recognize such unit beings or "things" in nature; we could not bestow this quality upon them did we not possess it, nor could we recognize it at the base of our "I am I" if it were not really there. As has been so forcibly pointed out by Lotze:

"No twisting of imagination, or subtlety of argument, can show how a mind not really one could appear to itself at all; or break the strength of the conviction inwrought into the very structure of self-consciousness, that the real and spiritual being, which we call Mind, is not a fortunate confluence or phenomenal center of changing modes, but a unit-being, and a reason of all unity in whatever becomes the object of its thought."*

*Loc. Cit., p. 687.

Nor does this recognition of a real unit, an "I am myself," ever vary, from the cradle to the grave. Through pain and grief, in joy or gladness, in youth or age, though means after means of communication with externals be cut off by disease or old age, through every conceivable mental change of opinion or belief, the "I am I" is equally undisturbed. The connection between soul and body must be absolutely severed by insanity (disease) or death for this center of consciousness to cease to recognize itself upon this plane, even as a real, abiding unity. Every state of consciousness is constantly referred to this "I" as its base, as the subject which experiences the state. A mental self-conscious state not involving an "I" at its base is absolutely unthinkable.

In this "I," thus shown to be necessary to self-conscious existence, there are many other attributes, besides those we have been studying, incapable of arising out of any combination of sense-perceptions, and which must therefore be inherent to or potential within itself. One such is memory. This is a reproduction in consciousness, not only of things not there, but of things which never were there. For the things we perceive through our senses are not stored up in the brain even as infinitesimally small pictures or representations, for they never reach our brain as such. It is only the effects of these, recorded in molecular changes, which are thus stored, and the mind in remembering has to take these old effects, connect them with their old causes, and from this construct the old representation. Truly, this is a creative process, requiring a creative center of consciousness, and a center which can only exercise this power through its being one in essence with creative consciousness in nature. It requires an abiding, permanent "I," or the picture could not be recognized as belonging to a past experience. As has been pointed out by Prof. Ladd:

"It is a fact of consciousness, on which all possibility of connected experience and of recorded and cumulative human knowledge is dependent, that certain phases or products of consciousness appear with a claim to stand for [to represent] past experiences to which they are regarded as in some respect similar. It is this peculiar claim in consciousness which constitutes the essence of an act of memory; it is this which makes memory wholly inexplicable as a mere persistence or recurrence of similar impressions. It is this which makes conscious memory a spiritual phenomenon, the explanation of which, as arising out of nervous processes and conditions, is not simply undiscoverable in fact, but utterly incapable of approach by imagination. When, then, we speak of a physical basis of memory, recognition must be made of the complete inability of science to suggest any physical process which can be conceived of as correlated with that peculiar and mysterious *actus* of the mind, connecting its present and its past, which constitutes the essence of memory."[*]

Again, memory proves a unit center because each soul remembers its own experiences only. It cannot encroach upon those of another, which would be the case if there were any general remembrance possible in nature. No chasm can be more abrupt or impassible than the line which divides conscious experiences; and no theory will account for this except that of permanent, conscious unit-centers or souls. It is granted that impressions are registered not only in the brain, but in every tissue of the body as well, for each organ has its memory, but—

"For that spiritual activity which actually puts together in consciousness the sensations, there can not even be suggested the beginning of a physical explanation."[†]

---

[*]Loc. Cit., p. 558. [†]Loc. Cit., p. 556.

This is to be found in a unifying center, or soul, alone. Memory, then, is a conscious reproduction by a permanent center of consciousness, an "I am myself," of past experiences. Especially will this be apparent when the relation of will to memory is considered. We consciously and deliberately will to reproduce past events—an impossible process were there not within us the subject of those experiences we will to recall.

In the Will, also, we find a power native to the soul, and one unthinkable except as the action of a conscious entity. As well predicate thought without a Thinker as will without a Willing Entity. This faculty is entirely without a physical basis, or at least it has no physical organs, but pervades the entire structure of the body, apparently as the agent of an inner, controlling essence. Nor is an organ necessary; for the simple, homogeneous speck of protoplasm known as the *amœba*, structureless and entirely destitute of organs, exercises this faculty undeniably in those changes it makes "which can not be wholly explained by reference to any change in its environments." Its superiority to and control over the body as a purely physical mechanism is shown by the fact, pointed out by Duchenne, and others, that the will is the very first agent to act upon restored nerve fibers after their injury. It is the active agent of consciousness in selecting what sensations and perceptions, among the vast number continuously clamoring for the soul's attention, shall be attended to. It can even change the very reports, so to speak, of those sense organs, upon whose action materialism would fain have us base its coming into existence. Willing, too, is a purely mental activity. No passing-over of force from spiritual to physical realms accompanies its action. There is positively no physical energy expended in willing. All the apparent effort is entirely the result of the physical mechanism carrying out, or attempting to carry out, the mandates of the will, as pronounced by the Ego.

Like the memory, too, the will is always specialized. There is no general willing; it can only act with a definite object. Its sole material connection is that when a fiat of the will issues certain molecules, associated with the line of action willed, move. But this shows an extraneous mover. It is a physical correlation of molecules with an act of consciousness; not an origination in such motion of either will or consciousness. Were there no other evidence, the undoubtedly genuine cases of recovery from deep-seated diseases under the action of the will would be sufficient to show that it is either the agent of the mind, or the mind itself, in activity, and quite superior to the physical body which it controls. It is true that, primarily, acts of the will arise out of sensations and perceptions depending upon environment; but the choosing among these of the particular perception or sensation to which the attention shall be directed is a new element, which can not be relegated to mere experiences, or a combination of any other mental activities. It is a deliberate choice of a tool by an artisan having more than one at his disposal.

For if we examine these very sensations themselves, which materialism claims have arisen out of mechanical motion among physical molecules, we find that they are located in the mind itself, and not in the body. They evade all attempts to reduce them to the domain of physics by measurement. There is no standard in all molecular physics to determine the amount of sensation involved in a "severe" pain or a "highly pleasurable" feeling. Being activities of the mind alone, and only correlated with, not transmuted from, molecular activities, they can only be expressed in terms of consciousness, not in those of physics.

We have several sense organs, also, each carrying a distinct class of impressions to the mind. To synthesize these widely varying activities into a harmonious whole, recognized by the "I am I" as its experiences, requires that this "I am I" should be separate from and superior to any one or all of them. And upon this ability to associate different classes of sensations is built the mind's power to project and locate in space those objects which its sense-organs bring into its environment. The sensations themselves can not be extended within the brain; it requires a power potent in the soul itself to project into space certain sensations depending, as has been pointed out, upon molecular activities entirely unlike them in action and essence. The presence of this synthesizing center is shown unquestionably by the fact that a synthesis does take place—that two or more distinct sensations are unified in the mind as one object. Were there not this synthesizing center, different senses, such as sight, hearing and touch, might all report the same object; but how could any knowledge arise that all these reports referred to the same thing without a synthesizer? Except for synthesis, also, there could be but one sensation at a time actively present in a consciousness compounded only of varying states. And were there but one sense organ, which would be practically the case if but one could act at once, our concepts of time and space would be so changed that we would be as unlike our present selves as an oyster, whose consciousness, indeed, must be largely similar to that which ours would be under such circumstances.

Sensations and ideas are themselves only phenomena, and not entities. It is impossible, therefore, for a sensation to be the subject of its own states; there is absolutely required an entity for this purpose. Nor can any reason be given why motion should become sensation. It is not a product of evolution   As pointed out by Prof. Ladd:

"That I am affected with a certain sensation of color, lying at the bottom of the spectrum's scale, when several billion vibrations of ether strike the retina, and with a qualitatively different sensation when the number of vibrations is increased by several billions more, cannot be explained as an evolution. The same remark holds within the limits of each of the other senses. Their scales of quality are not such that experiences at one place of the scale can be evolved from those at other places of the scale. Some of them, such as smell and taste, do not admit of being referred to any form of a scale diagram representing relations of quality. The feeling of heat is not another phase of the feeling of cold; neither of the feelings of temperature is to be explained as arising out of feelings of pressure or motion."*

It is quite evident, too, that the senses restrain and limit the powers of the Ego. As observed by Plato, "The soul reasons best when least harassed by the senses." There are evidently more "things" than senses, as is shown in many ways; notably, in the world of effects lying just outside the colors of the spectrum, and of which our senses afford us no intimation. Finally, if the sense organs were the result of outer stimuli there could never happen, as is the case with every organized being now, the construction of sense organs in entire absence of the stimuli held to be a necessary antecedent to their appearance. Every child

---

*Loc. Cit.

at birth comes into the world with perfectly formed eyes
which have never known the stimulus of light, and so on,
although in a lesser degree, with all its sense organs.   It
is no explanation to say that these have been primarily so
organized, and are now transmitted by heredity; for the
very first step in their acquirement, no matter how small,
has always and necessarily been taken in the silence and
darkness of subjective being.   The outer stimuli have only
aroused the inner response; they have not created, nor can
they create, evolve, nor even modify, this.

Of course, we shall be met here with the materialistic
assertion that, as the vegetable kingdom, even, shows
traces of nerve functions, and as this proceeds upward
through the apparently structureless *amœba* to the highly
complex system of man, increasing in conscious functioning with each increase of specialization, sensation is thus
plainly a product of evolution.   Yet the functions of the
simplest nervous system are unique.   Nothing in the
whole curriculum of physical science affords even a working hypothesis by which to explain or account for the appearance of the conscious factor.   Until some reasonable
attempt is made to explain how motion becomes sensation,
occult theories must take precedence; especially as these
are in full accord with the facts.   These teach that the
outer sense organ is constructed by and because of the
inner impulse of consciousness seeking expression in form,
in order to bring about sense relations on the material plane
—the only relation possible at the present stage of the
soul's becoming; and that so far from consciousness arising
mechanically out of these sense organs, they actually
limit and inhibit conscious manifestations.   There is a
continuous effort for more consciousness to function than

the sense organ affords opportunity for, which fact is the very base and causal antecedent of all so-called evolution, were science not too blind to perceive it. But he who starts in the wrong direction travels a weary journey; and until scientists cease to seek in material phenomena for the origin of consciousness they can only increase their distance from the truth by any apparent progress they may make.

To return: Of ideas arising out of sensations it can only be affirmed that they are modes of activity of the Ego, not of any conceivable physical juxtaposition of molecules. The laws governing the association of ideas are to be found in the nature of the soul itself. They can not be derived from any known behavior of so-called physical atoms. They are *sui generis;* and, while undoubtedly correlated with, do not nor can not arise out of, the molecular activities of the brain because of the impassible gulf shown to exist between motion and sensation. Their origination is inexplicable unless we admit the presence of an observing entity, or soul. Ideas can not associate themselves; and while they may arise semi-mechanically in an idle brain, the case is quite different when the aroused Ego, through its will, asserts not only what ideas shall arise in the mind, but the manner of their association as well.

All material ideas having their root in sensations are conscious relations of the Ego to the material plane, conditioned upon its material organ. They are in no way similar to the Ego's consciousness of self, or of its own being. The mind or thinking Ego never applies the terms of sensation arising out of its relations with external nature to its own being; it never thinks of itself as

"large" or "small," or as "hot" or "cold."   Nothing could
be more definite than the line drawn between its own native and proper functions and those arising out of its association with the sense organs of the body.   And so entirely dependent is sensation upon the soul that clear
vision and acute hearing, etc., depend for their nicety not
upon perfect sense organs—though these are necessary
accessories,—but upon a clear mental interpretation of
what is seen or heard.

Again, if consciousness were a transmutation, in some
inconceivable manner, of molecular into psychic activities
within the brain, then there ought to be both a specialization of nerve substance and a constant ratio between the
brain and mind.   But, as Prof. Ladd states:

"So far as we know anything about the particular molecular activities of the central nervous system which are most directly connected
with the phenomena of consciousness, they do not differ essentially
from other molecular activities of this system not thus connected
with consciousness. The chemical constitution and structural form
of the nerve-fibers and nerve-cells of the brain do not differ from
those of the spinal cord in any such respect as, of itself, to account
for the difference in the relations in which the two stand to conscious
mental states. They do not so differ even from the molecules which
enter into the living plant or animal, of much lower species, mentally,
than man."[*]

Thus there is evidently no physical evolution of the
ganglionic cells after they have reached a certain point.
The most profound philosopher is using cells of the same
kind to relate him to sensuous existence as his Darwinian
"cousin," the ape.   There ought to have been a further
and most marked specialization of form and structure if
mental activities had been evolved from increasing nerv-

Loc. Cit.

ous complexities. Instead of this, there is only an entirely relative—not absolute—increase in the amount of
these cells. Is it not evident that "gray matter" is only
the pigment, as it were, with which the ape makes his
feeble conscious daubs, while man produces magnificent
paintings because the pigment in his case is in the hands
of superior intelligence?

There is often, too, the most marked divergence between
mental and physical evolution. The human child comes
into the world perfectly mindless as far as anything beyond reflex action is concerned, yet it is possessed of a
most perfect and elaborate nervous system, "far surpassing
that of the most intelligent adult animal." Where is the
mental activity which ought to have unavoidably accompanied this physical evolution, if the one process arises
out of the other? In the first year of the child's life,
mental activity makes the most wonderful strides, running
far ahead of its supposed physical source. The same in-
equality attends their relations throughout life. Especially is it marked in old age, where, long after the physical
has ceased to progress, and is even rapidly retrogressing,
the mind retains all its pristine vigor. Of course, this is
seen only in cases of men who have lived a mental life. A
man who has passed his existence as an ambulating vegetable decays like one; he has no mind to shine forth
amidst the ruins of his body. But the presence of a vigor-
ous mentality connected with great physical decrepitude in
but one case proves its possibility in all. Cases of illness
with mental vigor are in point here—in fact, many diseases, by refining and subduing animality, actually increase mentality. Of course, there is a golden mean, and
bodily age or disease to the point of cutting off the Ego's

hold upon its sense organs must be followed by their ceasing to give evidence of its presence.   In such cases mental decrepitude apparently follows upon the physical. But, as already pointed out, there can be no argument drawn from this intimate dependence upon the body by the soul for its conscious relations with this plane against its actual and independent existence.   Every entity in nature is dependent upon other entities; the very cells of man's body are made up of countless lives, having their own life history beyond and outside of this association, upon which, nevertheless, they entirely depend.   The Ego within the body shows more numerous and important phenomena to entitle it to be claimed as a real unit entity than do any or all physical phenomena on the part of the latter; and if either is to be declared non-existent, it must, by all the laws of logic, be the body, and not the soul.

But the crowning physiological argument in favor of a soul is in the nature of consciousness itself, and that, as has been pointed out, all its higher spiritual activities can neither be connected with any definite material organ nor proven to arise out of any conceivable mode of molecular motion within the brain.

"For all the higher spiritual faculties," says Lotze, "which consist in judgment of the relations of given conceptions, we neither know how empirically to demonstrate a definite bodily organ, nor should we know how to conceive precisely what such an organ could contribute toward the solution of the most essential part of the problem —that is, the pronouncing of the judgment itself.   It is conceivable, on the other hand, that these higher activities might presuppose the complete and clear representation of the content about which the judgment is to be passed, and, consequently, also the undisturbed function of those organs which contribute, first, to perception by the senses; then to its reproduction and combination with other perceptions; and, finally, to the appropriate attachment of feelings of value to each of them."*

Yet this "clear representation of the content about which the judgment is to be passed" must not be conceived of as taking part in the judgment itself. This would land us in the materialistic absurdity of supposing that all the activities of consciousness were only the product of the molecular associations concerned in their representation. As well try to identify the bile as a real physical secretion of hypochondria, or tears as liquid sorrow.

In this connection, too much stress can not be laid upon the importance of the unity of consciousness (before referred to), of the Ego, or soul. All our mental faculties are but modes of its behavior. Its presence and native powers are demonstrated by its phenomenal activities. It would be less unphilosophic to deny the existence of electricity than of the center of consciousness at the base of the soul; for all we know concerning the former is drawn entirely from its objective phenomena, while of the latter we have in addition to these its subjective phenomena as well. And although the mental states, perceptions and sensations may be and are innumerable, they are alike referred to the one subject—the "I" upon which they all rest. Is it a thinkable proposition that the whole possible gamut of conscious experiences could be thus unified in a subject of them all without the real and actual existence of that subject?

"To have a variety of changing states attributed to it as the subject of them all—this is to demonstrate in consciousness a claim to real being. Unchanging rigidity, the permanence of the mathematical

---

*Loc. Cit., p. 558.

point or of the material atom, on the supposition that the latter undergoes no interior changes whatever, if such rigidity and permanence anywhere exist, constitutes no claim to the title of real being.

"The soul exists in reality, above all other kinds of being, because it alone, so far as we know on good evidence, knows itself as the subject of its own states; or, indeed, knows the states of which it is the subject as states belonging to itself. But its law is that of development; and, unlike all 'things' which are subjects of various kinds of evolution, so called, the soul can recognize the law of its own being. When, therefore, we are asked what the mind really is, we can respond by telling what it comes to be as the result of its unfolding under the fixed conditions of its native powers. But these 'powers' cannot be called native, as though they were actual achievements of the mind's inborn faculties, or separate forms of energy inherent in it, after the analogy of the forces said [somewhat unintelligibly, it must be admitted,] to be 'inherent' in the atom.

"But we do not define the nature of any real being simply by stating how it appears and behaves in its most germinal and undeveloped form. The tree explains the seed; the adult bird, the egg; the character of the highly differentiated product must be studied in order to know the full description of the energies that are potential in the simple stages. It is an undoubted fact that the mind [soul] has a history in each individual case; and in each case such history is a development. This self-recognizing unity of development which belongs to the mind is a striking proof of the validity of its claim to be considered a real being. As the being which acts and knows itself as acting, which is acted upon and knows itself affected, which is the subject of states and itself attributes these states to itself, which develops according to a plan and so remembers and comprehends the significance of the past states that it can recognize the fact of its own development—as such a being the mind [soul] is more entitled to consider itself 'real' than to consider real any of the various objects that, immediately or indirectly, appear before it in the course of its history."*

*Loc. Cit., p. 680.

There is still another faculty of the mind which is, if possible, even more undiscoverable in and unrelated to any definite physical basis than those heretofore considered. This is that aspect or phase of consciousness known as the Feelings. Just what feeling consists in escapes definition. It is an innate, underived power of consciousness. It accompanies all sensation and all ideation, while it itself may be and often is experienced independently of any other conscious state. It is therefore, upon this plane at least, a basic aspect evidently of consciousness, if not the very essence of this itself. For all sense of personal identity may be lost, as in chloroform narcosis; all thought may cease, as in *yoga* or other concentration; all will may be suspended, as in the passivity of mediumship; or these may be annulled or suspended together in moments of terror, surprise, joy, or pleasure. Yet, untouched by all, burns the steady light of a conscious center which feels that it exists, or, rather, that it IS. That feeling is related to this plane by the sense organs is evident. That it is modified as to its states by these, follows as a necessary corollary, else there would be no reason for or even possibility of the association; but that it arises, *de novo*, out of any possible combination of merely fortuitous molecular activities is simply absurd. It measures all sensation, as to whether it is painful, pleasurable, or neutral (if such a state can exist); it equally accompanies thought, and classifies this by its own inherent analytical powers as belonging to or connected with one or other of the higher activities of the mind, such as imaginative, religious, moral, esthetical, etc. It binds all the other faculties of the mind into an unity such as is unexplainable except as the conscious functioning of a

self-conscious Ego. Feeling accompanies all possible experience. Whether one hate or love, whether he live in
intellectual realms or those of sensuous emotions, feeling
accompanies each state so faithfully that the only explanation of this is that it is the presence of a self-conscious
soul, exercising an underived and underivable power innate in consciousness itself, and hence a ray from or an
aspect of the Causeless Cause, in its finite manifestation.

All the evidence thus adduced to prove the presence of
a soul as a necessary deduction from physiological phenomena must not be understood as asserting or even in-
dicating that this soul is capable of being analyzed and its
nature explained, because we can prove its existence.
There is no phenomenon, nor entity, nor being in the
universe which does not at last escape analysis by disappearing in the great Unknowable Source of All, the
Causeless Cause. But it would seem the height of unphilosophic reasoning to admit the reality of the fleeting
and illusionary beings which constitute our bodies, together with their environments, and then to deny the real
existence of the conscious and permanent base, the
Knower, Observer and Recorder of this illusory experience. An Unknowable must always be admitted as an
ultimate factor; the finite can never hope to contain or
measure the Infinite, but we must beware that in our
ignorance we do not relegate to this Unknowable problems which belong only to the Unknown, and which it is
vital to our progress, and even our very existence, that
we discover.   To this Unknown which must be discovered
belong evidently inquiries such as we have been considering, as well as all phenomena which relate to the existence
of the soul, the modes of its behavior, the things which retard, prevent or accelerate its progress through the Cycle
of Necessity in which it has its present being.

CHAPTER II.

THE PSYCHOLOGICAL EVIDENCE OF THE EXISTENCE OF THE SOUL.

IN the preceding chapter attention has been paid to the evidences of a soul in the psycho-physiology of the waking state, or that of normal consciousness. No reference was had to the large and fertile field consisting of man's dreaming consciousness, together with the allied phenomena of trance, hypnotism, clairvoyance, and super-sensuous states generally.

It is evident that if there be a psycho-physiology of the waking state, there must also be one of sleep. As this occupies one-third of our entire existence, it cannot be safely ignored in any psychological investigation. It is hardly reasonable, in view of the wonderful utilization of every opportunity by nature, to infer that sleep is only intended for that bodily rest and recuperation to which it has been assigned by science. Furthermore, the so-called abnormal phenomena of trance, clairvoyance, thought transference, etc., representing a large" unclassified residuum" of psychic phenomena, have a most important bearing upon the question of human consciousness functioning independent of the body, and hence upon the existence of a soul.

There are also further facts and generalizations to be drawn from the study of the nature of the relation of consciousness to the human organism in particular, and to biological evolution in general, which may, perhaps, be profitably studied in connection with and as a preface to the consideration of dreaming and other supersensuous phenomena.

Taking up, primarily, then, these general considerations, we find a soul directly pointed at by the fact of self-consciousness. While consciousness of some degree necessarily accompanies every step of evolutionary development, in man alone it first reaches the condition of self-consciousness, or consciousness of consciousness. Man analyzes and examines his own consciousness. Now, analysis requires two factors—an analyzer and the thing analyzed. Therefore, self-consciousness implies most conclusively that man has become at least dual in his nature; that something has been added above and beyond the animal consciousness (which knows no "I") of the kingdom below him. One constituent of his being steps aside and critically examines other constituents. Unless his consciousness is dual and separable, it is incapable of this. No molecular motion—the materialistic source of thought and consciousness—can isolate itself and observe the mechanical details to which it owes its own existence. Such a process is inconceivable. As we have seen, only a soul independent of its physical sense organs for its conscious existence can satisfy the conditions of the problems of self-consciousness and self-analysis.

Further consideration shows us, also, that self-consciousness does not exhaust its peculiar and proper object, which is self. If consciousness were the product of the chemico-vital processes going on within the body, it ought, as the mere expression of this, to express it fully. It would be a simple question in mathematics—a case of two and two making four. Instead of this, our ordinary consciousness finds itself occupying a body of which it knows next to nothing. Our ordinary consciousness take notice. That there is an inner consciousness, or soul, and that this soul is intelligently conscious of every process going on within the body, is abundantly proven by recent experiments in hypnotism. This state, in which the ordinary consciousness is suspended to a greater or lesser degree and an inner permitted to function, shows that a very illiterate, ignorant person will display a familiarity with the anatomy and physiology of his or her organism, and a recognition of diseased conditions together with a knowledge of the remedies necessary to their alleviation or cure, far exceeding that of the most learned and experienced physician. That this information and knowledge proceed from an inner source, and are not due to thought transference or suggestion on the part of the physician, is proven by unsuspected physical conditions thus described having been verified by *post mortem.* This strange phenomenon can only be accounted for by admitting to man a higher consciousness than that which functions on the ordinary or waking plane, and which consciousness can only exist as the functions of an independent Ego, or soul.

It is true that self-prescribing, etc., are only comparatively low planes of the conscious functioning of the soul, but this does not diminish their real significance. The point made clear by them is that normal, waking consciousness expresses only a portion—a very small portion, in reality—of the conscious powers of the soul. The fact that the soul is superior to the body, and its conscious area actually limited by the sense organs of the latter, is thus firmly established.

If, also, we examine the relation sustained by consciousness to biological processes in general we shall find that the same conditions obtain. The manifestation of divine consciousness in physical form, which constitutes nature as we perceive it, is likewise limited in its expression by its material vehicle. There is a constant struggle on the part of the inner consciousness to express itself more fully and harmoniously than the "matter" with which it is associated permits. This fact is the sole agent in and the cause of all evolution. Both man and nature are constantly trying to displace this movable threshold of consciousness which they have in common. This threshold, the point of unstable equilibrium in nature, is the battlefield wherein every contest between "matter and spirit" takes place. Here the outer form is slowly modified by the continuous efforts of the inner consciousness, seeking a more perfect vehicle for its expression. The fact that modification is possible in man and nature prophesies in both, also, unlimited potentialities of future development.

And, truly, a biological process is only possible by means of a higher or transcendental consciousness in nature. If we take any division—the vertebrates, for example—we shall find the designing idea always precedes in time its evolution in matter. The intention of nature is plainly foreshadowed in the notochord, which still persists in some of the lower vertebrates; and the prophecy of this insignificant notochord finds its realization in the magnificent elaboration of the vertebral column, with its cranial enlargement, muscular, nervous, arterial, lymphatic, digestive, and other accessory systems, which together constitute the body of the being declared to be "a little lower than the angels in heaven." Yet science would have us believe that this wonderful result is due alone to the blind groping of natural forces under the impelling influence of unintelli-

gent law! Nay, if there were no other proof of there being a higher consciousness in nature and in man, it is
shown beyond all doubt by the very facts upon which
materialistic science chiefly relies—those of evolution.
No building was ever yet constructed whose model or design was not previously present in the consciousness of its
architect, and no biological process ever took place which
was not previously present in the mind of a Higher Intelligence.

Evolution continuously displaces the threshold of consciousness in nature and in man. And biology, also,
shows that for the whole of organic nature, including man,
there are two increasingly unequal divisions—that part
which sense organs disclose, and that portion which is
transcendental to or beyond sensuous perception. For
an oyster most of the world is transcendental; that man's
consciousness is very much widened in area does not by
any means imply that he is in contact with the whole of
nature. Step by step, the higher consciousness has
evolved organs capable of relating itself to larger and
larger areas of contact with external things.

The design in each instance has preceded the construction of the thing designed. If the brain, for example,
were developed by blind force alone, how could it have
been adapted for future needs? Yet all the functions of
the human mind, all its god-like faculties, were foreseen
and provided for in anticipation by the first swelling
which, at one extremity of an otherwise indistinguishable
line of nerve substance, prophesied and promised the
magnificent display of will, intellect, reason, emotion and
intuition subsequently enabled to manifest through the
brain of a Spencer or a Shakespeare. And the un-

broken sequence of design and thought lie before our eyes all our lives, yet we are asked to believe that fortuitous chance caused force to take this direction; that all this is but the sum of the molecular and chemical action of blindly working law!

This movable and moving threshold of consciousness, then, appears in all nature. It can only be the result of two causes. Either an inner and a higher consciousness is shaping and transforming matter, with a definite and intelligent end in view, or it is the result of blind chance working under the despotic need of unintelligent force. And if we are compelled to admit an inner and a higher consciousness in any single effort of nature, the fortress is taken; for, step by step, we shall be forced to admit a higher consciousness in all; and the question as to whether man has a higher consciousness, or soul, is answered by the biological argument in the affirmative. And again we are driven to the conclusion that, since this higher consciousness is not dependent in any way upon the matter which it shapes to further its ends—as a potter might—for its continued existence, then it does not, and indeed can not, die upon the death or transformation of the latter. On the contrary, analogy points to the fact that, as a man wears out and renews his body, cell by cell, many times in the labors of a life, so his soul must wear out and renew many bodies in the course of its infinite pilgrimage. Here, once again, then, the fact of and reason for reincarnation meets us squarely as the logical result of biological necessities.

Again, the evolution of sense organs and the widening of consciousness upon this plane are parallel. Nor is it probable that man will evolve any absolutely new sense

organ which will relate him to new phenomena or facts of
nature. But this is not necessary, since those he has are
capable of almost infinite expansion along lines they now
subtend. And that no new physiological organs are in
process of evolution points plainly to the inference that
future development must be in psychic or mental directions. This will certainly be the case unless we refuse to
predicate any further advance as possible to the human
Ego—a conclusion to which the egotism of self-satisfaction
is very prone.

If one wears blue glasses all nature assumes a blue hue.
Materialism has looked at the universe so long through
material lenses that it has become spiritually color blind.
It also confounds the condition of thinking with the cause
of thought; it mistakes the physical brain, which is the
battery by means of which the operator beyond transmits
thought messages to this physical plane, for the creator of
that which it merely transmits. It is exactly the same as
if a countryman were to insist that the instrument which
ticks off his message is the source of the intelligence displayed.

Self-consciousness, then, together with its varied functions, such as reflective thought, constructive imagination,
volition, even to the extent of deliberately abandoning
the body by suicide—all show that that body is occupied
and controlled by a soul almost infinitely superior to it in
function and powers; and, as a necessary corollary, that the
soul has acquired this undoubted superiority by an almost
numberless series of reincarnations.

A careful examination must convince any one that
thought comes into the consciousness ready made; that is,
that we do not consciously create it, but receive it as

though transmitted to us from some source outside or beyond us. From a perception of this, poets have always claimed to be inspired by a "muse." This reception of completed thought shows plainly that the physical brain is only an organ to relate thought to the physical plane, and not to create it in any sense of the word. The whole of nature's so-called creative processes are simply unconscious thought—that is, unconscious to us. Could we attune our consciousness to that of the creative intelligences in nature, we would know what is going on in the mind of an ant, as also in the mind of a flower or stone. And that the soul is so attuned, in a degree at least, is proven by the fact that in deep hypnotic states it knows nature's thoughts or processes going on within its own physical organism, and can and does recognize and prescribe for diseased conditions therein. This is just in accordance with what must be predicated of soul, which, being independent of the body for all except one class of purely material functions, and which, passing from body to body by means of reincarnation, must accumulate an amount of conscious experiences, with knowledge and wisdom arising therefrom, which cannot of necessity find full and complete expression in any one body, as a small engine is insufficient to afford full expression for the energy of a series of boilers. To turn on the full force would in both instances be to destroy the vehicle.

Proceeding, next, more directly to the examination of the dreaming and other abnormal states of consciousness, we note, as a basic parallel, that the projection of images during sleep is exactly equivalent to perception in the waking state, both placing objectively something we perceive subjectively. A tree, for example, is not seen actually where it is; nor is its size nor color nor any of its attributes perceived externally. The perception is entirely internal; the location and definition of the object externally is an after operation belonging to experience and judgment. A blind man, suddenly restored to sight, as has been done by operation, is at first utterly unable to estimate the distance, perspective, and other qualities of objects, except as the result of painfully acquired experience, in which perception plays no further part than to furnish the primary data. Therefore, there is, *ipso facto*, nothing in dreams which excludes their phenomena from the domain of actual perception. As continuously occurs in waking life, these perceptions may be wrongly interpreted; but they are none the less true perceptions, and have their psycho-physiology, our ignorance of which is no warrant for its non-existence.

Waking consciousness is the result of an almost infinite number of physical stimuli reaching perception and recognition by means of the sense organs. In dream, the soul responds to stimuli from inner and more spiritual planes. The senselessness of most remembered dreams is due to a mixing of the waking and dreaming states, when objective stimuli are partly dramatized on the subjective plane, and *vice versa*. In ordinary dreams all stimuli are dramatized; thus resembling somewhat a play where the actors are limited to pantomime for the expression of their ideas. And the causes of the dramatization not being perceived, the judgment necessarily rests on false premises. The waking state is partly objective and partly subjective; dream is the same—only between the two states the threshold of consciousness is greatly displaced. In the waking condition the consciousness is engrossed by the

stronger stimuli of physical life, and the subjective threshold recedes accordingly. In dream the objective threshold recedes, and the consciousness responds to an entirely different class of stimuli, of a subjective nature. It
is not claimed that these minor stimuli are not present in
the waking condition. They are; but are crowded out of
the attention, or displaced by the stronger. They resemble a feeble chord in music so lost in louder and higher
pitched ones that we are unaware it is being sounded.
It is only as objective stimuli fade or are suppressed that
we can become conscious on subjective planes. In both
sleeping and waking states it is, of course, the same consciousness, but responding to different stimuli.

If, then, the physiology of dreams carries perception
and consciousness to the dream plane, the importance of
studying this and its allied unconscious (so called) conditions cannot be overestimated. For once we show that
ordinary dream and the higher dream states, such as
somnambulism and trance, are merely gradations of the
same consciousness responding to new stimuli; we not
only establish the fact of another consciousness than the
waking, but we also prove that this consciousness is very
greatly superior to the waking, in knowledge, functions,
and power. In other words, we prove an inner Ego, or
soul.

In demonstration of this connection, if we pass but a
single step above the ordinary dream, and admit significant dreams as possible—and who does not?—we are in
contact with a consciousness which is capable of forewarn-
ing, or prophecy—powers far surpassing its waking capacities. Again, sleep-walking is but the dreamer acting
out the dramatization of his own dreams, as the writer,

who was in youth a somnambulist, can personally testify. Many, if not all, the phases of natural somnambulism are so plainly identical with those of induced somnambulism, or the hypnotic states, that we are enabled to connect these conditions beyond any doubt. And in the hypnotic or induced somnambulism, whether self-induced or due to the will of another, we forge the last and strongest link which binds the waking consciousness to one almost infinitely higher than itself, which is yet truly its own self, only functioning above and beyond the limitations of its material sense organs.

In studying dream, as the very lowest yet most universal of these states, we note the entrance of a most important factor, or the use by the dreaming consciousness of entirely new concepts of time and space. It is a well-known and admitted physiological fact that dreams which on the waking plane would require years of time for their enactment find on the dream plane that even a moment is sufficient for the dreaming consciousness to appreciate them in their most minute details. Thus De Quincey had one dream which apparently extended over some sixty years, but which actually occupied scarcely as many moments. Uxhill, also, on three successive nights, not only saw his whole life pass in review, but appreciated its moral bearing.*

Now, the fact that the relation of the thinking Ego to time conceptions is changed in dream is one whose importance cannot be overestimated. The exact speed at which objective stimuli are transmitted from the periphery to the brain centers is well known. In like manner, the time required by the consciousness to record visual perceptions is also subject to accurate measure-

*Du Prel, *Philosophie der Mystic.*

ment, as has been pointed out by Helmholtz, Fechner, and others. Since it is the same "I" which perceives both in the waking state and in dreams, and since perception in the waking state can only proceed at a definite, measurable rate of speed, if we find in dream this same "I" recording perceptions at a rate a million times greater than that which its physical organ, or brain, is capable of registering, it follows that it can not be using this physical organ, and is therefore not limited to the latter for its manifestations of consciousness. This alone proves that we possess a consciousness independent of the body, and, therefore, a soul, beyond all cavil or dispute.

Of the nature of dreams are the cases of partial drowning, where the whole life of the individual passes in review, to its most minute detail, during the brief interval in which the higher consciousness is permitted to function through the suppression of the lower by the physical asphyxiation and psychic exaltation which accompany the act. In the same category are the well-authenticated facts of the entire suppression of pain during the burning of both witches and martyrs. Through the tremendous psychic exaltation upon such occasions, the consciousness is transferred to higher, or soul, planes, and the body burns without giving the soul any concern; it feeling, in the supreme arousing of its faculties, that its existence is not dependent upon its body in any degree.

The power of the center of consciousness, or soul, to use differing vehicles for its manifestation is the key to all hypnotic and supersensuous states. It is their only rational explanation. For if the threshold of consciousness is displaced to any marked extent, or, in other words, if the center of consciousness which constitutes the human soul uses an inner vehicle, the new stimuli relate it to such unfamiliar phenomena that it often seems even to itself to be another consciousness—to belong to some other person. This has been well shown by the experiments of Binet and Janet, in France. In these, the permitting of the inner Ego to function through the suppression of the limiting sense organs by hypnosis caused an ignorant peasant woman, for example, to so widen her conscious area as to refuse to believe that she was identical with the stupid " Janet" of her ordinary, unhypnotized experience.

This non-recognition of the functions and powers of the soul accounts for most, if not all, the cases of "spirit guides" and " controls" in mediums and hypnotics; for the ordinary mediumistic or trance "control," or " guide," is only a case of self-hypnosis, where a dramatization of the inner consciousness takes on the part of such guide, adviser, or prevaricator, according as the medium or hypnotic rises to a higher or lower plane of his or her being.

It may be objected, in this relation, that these particular manifestations of the powers of the soul are morbid, because connected with morbid conditions. But this does not follow. As well hold the light which passes through a lens to be abnormal, and not really light, because the process of polishing and shaping the lens which permits of its being focused is unusual, or because the capacity to focus light is not a property of the stone in its natural condition.

All such phenomena must be carefully studied, analyzed, and classified by science before it can impose its dictum upon the results of investigations in regions which it

proudly refuses to enter. Nor can it be expected to lead
investigation or thought. It has always been the un-
relenting opposer of new ideas, as the new ideas in their
turn have always been the deadliest foes of the old. It
was scientific authority, as expressed in a little body of
men, who, having mastered the externals of existing
thought, and thus filled the measure of their own capacity,
railed when Harvey asserted that the blood circulated
through the human body ; when Stevenson foretold the
speed and usefulness of steam vehicles; and so on,
through a long list of similar counts; and which to-day
looks on with solemn discontent as the birds float through
the air in direct violation of its conceptions of the laws of
physics, dynamics and gravitation. For the same force,
applied in the same manner, and attached to the same
proportion of weight, when put into a " scientific" machine
refuses to fly. And yet no field is so full of proofs of
the existence and functioning of a divine soul as that
found in the marvelous collection of facts, and deductions of design and intelligence therefrom, which are the
result of scientific inquiry.

But whether or not man has a soul, it is evident that
he exhibits mental and spiritual powers which can not be
connected with nor explained by his material organism.
All the conscious aspects of his being are *sui generis*, and
not derivable in any manner from his material aspects.
Yet under the philosophic axiom that any law must necessarily be universal in its action to exist at all, this conscious energy which he exhibits must fall under the same
law of conservation which obtains on the material plane.
And this conservation of mental energy requires a
mental vehicle, and one capable of passing from body to

body upon the death of these; else the mental energy of one life is not conserved and carried over to the next, as its true conservation demands. Thus a reincarnating soul is directly pointed out and connected with the body by the two greatest generalizations of modern science—the conservation of force and the law of evolution. For either subjective energy, intellect, emotion, will, etc., are stored up in and transmitted under the law of force conservation by a soul, or this law, as well as that of evolution, is violated. Intelligence can only be conserved by intelligence, and its evolution thus lies necessarily along its own, or subjective, lines. In other words, the cause must be equal to the effect; and intelligence can only be the creation of and transmitted by intelligence. One sees at once how immense must be the waste of energy manifesting as intellect or intuition if the process of its evolution has to be begun anew with each new babe born on earth, to be again cut short by death when perhaps at its very highest evolutionary activity, unless that energy is carried forward from personality to personality by means of the repeated reincarnation of the soul. If, then, the energies of the soul obey, as they must, the law of force conservation, reincarnation becomes an absolute necessity.

There is another point overlooked by science. For intelligence to supervene upon unintelligent matter, under the play of blind force, demands as great an effort of the imagination and faith as the exploded theological theory of creation out of nothing. In the face of this, science has ever sought to find the source of intelligence in some nook or by-way of matter, forgetting that matter only shows the evidence of the presence of intelligence, not its underlying source. The key to the confusion lies in the

fact of subconscious thought, which is none the less
thought because acting below the plane of self-consciousness. Thought is of every plane in the Cosmos; the
very stones have their manasic principle. Thought and
organization go on side by side unconsciously until the
plane of self-consciousness is reached, when man suddenly becomes aware of both a thinking and a conscious
principle within him. This does not imply that either
. or both were absent on the planes below. Remember
that thought, as we have pointed out, comes into the
mind ready made, and is the ideation of the Higher
Ego, the *rationale* of which will be explained in the
chapter which deals directly with that subject. Meanwhile, it is plainly seen that the soul is conscious on
lower planes by self-prescribing, etc., and, in varying
degree, upon higher ones by clairvoyance and prophetic
vision.

When man's consciousness is limited to the coarser
stimuli transmitted by his physical senses, it can only
function on the physical plane. In this condition it is
termed the lower Ego, or personality. When these senses
are suspended by sleep, trance, or death, his consciousness
functions on interior and higher planes until again aroused,
by awakening, in the one case, and by reincarnation
in the other, to the old physical stimuli. This latter consciousness, which passes in sleep or death to purely spiritual planes, we term the Higher or true Ego, because it is
not limited by its physical envelope, is untouched by the
changes of state we know as birth and death, and transmits its constantly increasing increment of wisdom and
intelligence from body to body by means of its reincarnation. The threshold of physical consciousness is the

dividing line between the Higher Ego and lower personality. It embraces a large field of more or less confused
conscious states before it merges into the pure spiritual
consciousness of the Higher Ego, upon the one side, or
into the purely sensuous consciousness of the personality,
upon the other. As the physical senses and sensitive-
ness to the finer vibrations of astral matter constitute this
threshold, each man has of necessity a differing consciousness both of Higher Ego and lower personality from all
other men. Taken together, they represent the sum of the
wisdom and knowledge acquired throughout the entire
series of his rebirths, or reincarnations. The personal
consciousness is limited by the particular body it is in-
habiting. The body, again, is the result of the law of
cause and effect, running through the affinities which
govern its selection, and which Theosophy terms "karma,"
or sequence, or the unvarying succession of cause and
effect upon all planes, physical, pyschic, and intellectual.

If it be asked why man's personal consciousness has
not yet reached the point where he is sensible of these
finer forces, it is answered that the coarser the force the
quicker the evolution of the organ to express it. The
finer, more spiritual forces have not yet had biological
time to evolve organs, especially as it would seem that
this evolution must largely consist in rendering more
delicate and sensitive those man now possesses. By
these, the eye and ear are not so much referred to as
analogous organs for psychic and spiritual perception,
which man now possesses—at least in a rudimentary condition.

But the time will come, and in fact is now here for certain individuals of the race, when clairvoyance, thought

transference, intuition, and many other spiritual faculties will be as normal as is sense perception at present. They are simply natural faculties of man's Higher Ego, or soul, struggling into the domain of self-consciousness upon this plane. In this soul, or Higher Ego, is the true individuality, the real life, and consciousness. The personality is but the bundle of sense organs through which we gather experience and wisdom on the material plane, which is our present area of activity. The Higher Ego represents all that we have become since we assumed control of our own destinies.

The personality represents the amount of this stored wisdom which any particular body is capable of expressing; remembering that all bodies (sense organs) limit consciousness, instead of creating it. But this limitation falls under the universal law of cause and effect, and is therefore in each life brought about by the deeds of those of the past, as will be shown in the proper connection.

CHAPTER III.

THE EVOLUTION OF THE SOUL.

A STUDY of the evolution* of the human soul implies and necessitates a primary examination of the processes of evolution generally. Man is but a factor in nature—a part of the finite expression of the inexpressible Infinite—and differs only in degree from entities both above and below him in the scale of being. To arrive at his basic principles, to discover the *modus operandi* of the law of evolution under whose action he has reached his present standpoint, we have to turn to the universal cosmic factors which are equally the cause of man and of his every environment, whether material, intellectual or spiritual.

Certain recent experiments in physics, as well, also, as studies in mathematics, indicate hitherto unsuspected facts concerning natural phenomena, which have a profound bearing upon our conceptions of evolution. For instance: We have been taught by modern Western science to believe that force is most active and most potent upon grossly material planes, and that as we retreat to those more subjective it becomes less and less potent, until when mental or thought planes are reached it ceases to exist as force at all. Having passed the uttermost limits of our ability to pursue or detect it by physical means, it,

---

*The human soul can not be said to "evolve," in the scientific acceptation of this term, which is one-sided, as is most materialistic nomenclature. It is retained because convenient, and because its real meaning will be made clear in the context.

of course, no longer exists, unless we ascend to its higher retreats. Naturally, all experiments which deal with the purely physical seem to warrant this conclusion; especially those in which our very thoughts have been measured by molecular vibrations, expressed in a rise of temperature of the superficies of our brain, and which expression becomes more and more faint as our thoughts become more and more interior and subjective. But the behavior of water, even, when changed into vapor by heat, ought to have aroused suspicion that higher, states of matter contain greater potencies than lower. And the liberation of " inter-etheric" force by Keeley, backed by the behavior and potencies of electricity, together with numerous other phenomena, show us that what we have been in the habit of considering as the very essence of force is only the driftwood, so to speak, cast upon the shores of the great seas and oceans of potential energies in which we have our being.

Force being, like Substance and Consciousness, an attribute of the Absolute, must have infinite potencies. Hence, it logically follows that the nearer we penetrate to Absolute planes and eternal states of matter and consciousness the more stupendous and inconceivable become the forces which have there their normal field of activity. Nothing could exceed the emptiness, the utter void, in our conception of the interstellar or ethereal spaces lying between planets or suns. "Ether" has become a synonym for a state of matter which, while necessary to account for certain phenomena, is still considered so tenuous that it is practically non-existent, and hydrogen gas becomes by comparison with it as dense as iron. Yet out of this ether, when manipulated by knowledge, ap-

pears an energy before which all purely physical forces
are brushed aside, as are wisps of vapor in the path of a
cannon-ball. The only reason for the existence and relative permanency of the forces and matter of this plane
lies in the fact that they are out of direct relation to, and
only sustain those distantly harmonic with, the forces of
higher ones; that for astral, ethereal and akasic matter
our own "physical basis of life" is practically non-existent.
The ethereal vibrations play through our earth, our bodies
and our senses even, without producing any effect upon
our consciousness, or, as far as analogy permits us to suppose, our affecting by our presence the consciousness of
entities ensouled by this higher form of matter.

· Of course, this earth is not out of all relation to inner
states of matter and modes of force, but it is out of direct
relation thereto. Physical matter is the production of
forces having their origin in vibrations upon these interior
planes; but before such force is converted into physical
terms it passes through many gradations, each removing
it more and more from the potencies of those infinite
store-houses of energy from which the Cosmos springs
into being.

Bearing in mind, then, that force becomes more and
more potent as it retires to realms which to us are more
and more subjective, we can approach the subject of evolution with a better conception of the nature of the problems to be solved. For evolution is not, in this view, the
study of the process of "creation out of nothing"—the task
set themselves by theologians and theology-biased philosophers;—but, rather, the method by which the Absolute
or Infinite Force, Matter and Consciousness, limits itself
and becomes the finite as revealed to man. We are not

troubled at all by the insufficiency of the Cause, but by the apparent limiting in time and space of the effects of a necessarily unlimited Causeless Cause. One thing seems certain—that, as has been expressed by a recent writer,* "if Infinite Being is to be manifested in finite existence, it must be through infinite variations of the finite." The law of infinite variation, indeed, would seem to be one of the methods by which the Infinite expresses itself without lessening its own infinity. Another means by which, from our point of view, the Absolute and Unconditioned becomes the finite and conditioned, is in the all-pervading and unbroken law of cycles. In some form or degree, cyclic activity marks all existence or evolution, from that of a molecule to that of a manvantara.† Still another of these basic generalizations which have their common root in the Unknowable is the absolute sway of Cause and Effect in all realms of nature, from the highest and most super-spiritual to the lowest and most material. It is a logical conclusion that all absolutely unvarying laws, modes of motion, or states of consciousness, are direct aspects of the Absolute; and that by means of them we may approach to at least a partial conception of some planes of the Great Source of all life and being. Such would appear to be those we have cited; viz.: Infinite potentiality reflected in infinite variation of the finite; Absolute permanency of Being, shown in the absolute sway of Cause and Effect; and Eternal Duration in the unending, universal cycles which enable Duration to manifest as Time.

---

*Geometric Psychology.

†Manvantara—a period of universal objective existence followed by an equal period of (to us) unknowable subjective existence.

To the above, we have to add the unavoidable deduction that there can not be opposing factors in the
universe, whether existing as force, matter, or consciousness; because these would be either equal, and produce
universal inertia, or unequal, in which case the greater
must necessarily have overcome the lesser in the unthinkable durations of the eternities of the past.   An early
conception of the importance of this simple and logical
law, that unity in essence must underlie every manifestation in nature, however differentiated and opposed such
manifestations may appear, will clear away a mass of
theological rubbish from our first postulates, at the very
outset.   If all matter, force, and consciousness proceed
from unity, even though that unity remain for us an Unknowable Causeless Cause, still it effectually excludes the
possibility of evil as such from the cosmic scheme.   Hence,
Satans, Ahrimans, Beelzebubs, or Plutos are relegated to
realms of ignorance and fear in which they had their birth,
and good and evil become only relative aspects and planes
of the play of the absolute, impersonal law of Cause and
Effect.   ·
A study of evolution in general, then, is necessarily
prefaced by the admission or postulating of three great
Aspects of the one Unknowable Root, or Causeless Cause.
These are, as already pointed out, Consciousness, Substance, and Force.   Consciousness, often referred to as
"spirit," embraces all that manifestation of the Absolute
which we term subjective.   Substance is the root of all
matter and form, or the Object* side of nature, while
Force or Motion relates the one to the other and causes
all the bewildering complexity of form and function in the

*Cf. Secret Doctrine, Vol. I, page 16.

Cosmos. The absolute potentialities of Consciousness, Force, and Matter are and must ever remain infinite and unchanged. Yet the degree to which each is manifested in successive Universes must ever remain relative and finite. Hence, all the vast scheme of evolution which we perceive in nature is due solely to the correlations and combinations of these three Immutable and Universal Bases. We can not say, even at the end of a great manvantara, or the duration of a Universe, that anything has been added to the sum total of the Force, Consciousness, or Matter within the great Mother and Container of all—Space. Only their mutual relations have been somewhat changed. Consciousness, which before existed as an undifferentiated part of the Whole, has acquired Self-Consciousness, or a new quality or potency; but as Consciousness *per se* it remains unmodified. So of Force and Substance; they have been brought into newer and perhaps grander correlations, but as basic potentialities they remain unaltered. Nor can an end of this change of relation, or evolution as it appears to us, ever be predicated, for infinite potentialities of variation require infinite time for their manifestation. A dim conception of the possibilities of changes and of conscious experiences which never had a beginning, and of which no end can be predicated, may be had from a study of the law of permutation. The combinations possible with two elements are but two, but with three they rise to six; with four, to twenty-four; with five, to one hundred and twenty; and so on, ever increasing until we are driven to the recognition that an infinite series of atoms, such as are at the base of physical manifestation, even, must be capable of infinite combinations and correlations, and hence require infinite duration for that manifestation.

Approaching the survey of evolution from its material or Substance Aspect—the only one recognized by modern science—we may obtain a relative and limited idea of the manner in which matter takes on or descends into object-ive form by the following illustration:

Imagine a large vessel or receptacle filled with a solu-tion of some salt to the saturation point when heated to 100°. As long as this temperature is maintained the solution is perfectly transparent. No one would suspect any solid material hidden in its crystal clearness. But now let the rate of vibration be changed in the fluid; let the temperature fall to, say, 60°, and out of that which was before so clear, crystallizes a solid mass which renders the whole solution translucent, opaque, or it may so change its molecular relations as to cause it to become a solid.

From this comparison we may at least faintly conceive of that which transpires within the Universe at the dawn of a manvantara; for then Space may be likened to a clear, transparent, ethereal fluid, holding in potentiality the future Universe, which, so to speak, crystallizes out by a change of vibration within this universal, homo-geneous substance.

If we imagine matter as it exists upon our earth to pass into greater and still greater degrees of attenuation and dissociation—as, for example, when iron becomes gaseous —we will arrive ultimately at a state in which it is evenly distributed throughout the Cosmos, and subjected to con-ditions so different from any that now obtain, or at least that we can perceive, that we can no longer term it matter, but, rather, as approximating that eternal Substance, its (to us) subjective Root. To aid in forming some idea of the extreme attenuation and molecular dissociation to which matter in its cosmic condition is thus subjected, it is necessary to remember how minute the specks we know as planets are when compared to the space in which they revolve. The old illustration of Herschel as to the immense distances involved in visible space may aid us here:

Suppose one wished to construct a model of the solar system in which its proportions, though reduced, would be accurately preserved; and that for this purpose he should take a globe two feet in diameter to represent the sun. Then the earth, reduced to a corresponding size and in its proper position, would be represented by a pea placed at a distance of two hundred and fifteen feet from the globe; Jupiter, by an orange, placed a quarter of a mile away; and Neptune, our farthest planet, by a plum, at a distance of a mile and a quarter. On the same scale, Sirius, one of the brightest fixed stars, would be removed to the distance of forty thousand miles, so that it would require a space of nearly twice the entire circumference of the earth for a model to be constructed in which the earth is represented by a pea! Now, Sirius is not the nearest star; but the very closest one to our sun—Alpha Centaur—is 20,000,000,000,000,000 of miles distant, and within at least one-third of this vast extent of space our sun and his little band of planets represent all the visible matter, except a few wandering comets and systems of meteors.

We know matter in three states—solid, liquid and gaseous; and the experiments of Prof. Crooke prove a fourth state—that of " radiant matter"—as demonstrable to our senses. If beyond this fourth, or radiant, state we could imagine, if ever so dimly, the three following and still higher states, recognized and taught by Theosophy,

THE EVOLUTION OF THE SOUL.   63

we would have a dim conception of that original Substance out of which the material portion of this universe
is fashioned, when the dawn of a manvantara awakens it
once more to sentient life.

The infinite Universe, then, is filled, from a material
standpoint, with that which holds both the potency and
potentiality of matter. It also holds the potentiality and
potencies of spirit, or consciousness; being, besides, in
its aspect of ever-present, indestructible space, the arena
of that force which we know to be equally eternal under
its objectivized aspect of motion. Thus, at the dawn of
differentiation, at the beginning of the " out-breathing of
Brahm," or the manvantaric activity following the " in-
breathing" or universal pralaya, three hypostases of the Absolute—potential Matter, potential Thought, and potential Force—are held concealed, in some inconceivable way,
within the bosom of space, as our salt was also concealed
within the solution which we have used as a symbol.
And the material side of the Unknowable Triad is probably concealed in a precisely similar manner, or by the
rate of its vibration. For Theosophy accepts the matter
of science, and its force, or motion, also; but it avers,
most uncompromisingly, that the former is molded and
shaped by the latter through a third eternal predicate,
Intelligence, under the aspects of Consciousness and Ideation. Hence, when one great rhythm of the Universe has
expended its original impetus in a manvantaric objectiva-
tion, and has returned into the Silence and Darkness of
Non-Being until again at the initial moment of another
outward flow of the never-ceasing Motion, at this point
Intelligent Beings assume control, and, by ideative Will,
guide the vibrations of the eternal motion, so that matter

capable of exhibiting form appears as a consequence of this modification or change of vibration in the eternal Motion. Yet, as Absolute Force or Motion can not be added to nor diminished, so this modification of vibration must eventually be overcome, and the Universe return to its original condition, to again re-emerge in form when the reactionary swing of the pendulum of eternity has described its arc, and so permits of another effort on the part of these Creative Intelligences. Thus the law of cycles controls even this inconceivable period which measures the duration of an Universe. Like the intermittent glow of a fire-fly to one who watches the flight of the insect must appear even these vast successions of Universes to Intelligences behind the Veil of Isis, who remain forever untouched by any dissolution of form. At the outward flow of the eternal Motion, for them, nebulæ, suns and systems blaze into a fleeting existence; at the "inbreathing of Brahm" all disappear; and this in an eternal succession of exact cycles. These cycles, so transitory in eternity, are so vast in time that reason reels in the effort to conceive of them. The nature of the initiatory impress of these Formless Creative Intelligences from its conscious aspect is seen in the unerring selective "affinities" of atoms; from its force aspect it is undoubtedly a modification or change of vibration.

As the result of this primal modification of vibration, matter throughout the Universe assumes a state which the Book of *Dzyan*, quoted in the Secret Doctrine, describes as resembling "milk-white curds." These curds, which must be conceived of as infinitely more attenuated than the ether of science, are next brought by the agent through which cosmic intelligences act upon cosmic matter, known in Eastern Occultism as Fohat, into forms described as " fiery whirlwinds," or that in which magnetic attraction alone is controlling the vibration. Gravitation, representing a response to much lower rates of vibration and coarser aggregation of particles, only acts after the finer magnetic forces have prepared the necessary conditions permitting this form of attraction and repulsion to obtain a foothold among the sentient atoms. This stage in the evolution of matter up through the domain of that force we hazily describe as "magnetic," into the field where the lower activity of gravity obtains, may be traced in the form of some nebulæ, whose arrangement of matter still shows evidences of the original "whirlwind" force in the magnetic disposition of their contents.*

From the time of the evolution of matter into the nebulous condition, the after processes are comparatively easy to trace. Indeed, many of the subsequent evolutionary strides of Fohat are plainly visible within the limits of our own little solar system. The differing degrees of density from Neptune to Mercury; the state of matter in the sun; the dead moon, now in a minor pralaya, or rest; the comets which occasionally visit our region of space—all illustrate degrees of differentiation, and different states of

---

*One of the first discoveries made by means of the Lick telescope, at Mt. Hamilton, California, was this "whirlwind" disposition of the matter of some of the nebulæ. Prof. Holden, in an article contributed to a San Francisco journal, announced that "the arrangement of matter in some of these nebulæ was such as to indicate that *some other force than gravitation* had been concerned in its production." Science thus most unexpectedly confirmed the assertion, made some time previously by Madame H. P. Blavatsky, to the effect that if scientists had instruments sufficiently powerful to penetrate and resolve certain nebulæ they would discover that gravitation was not the universal force they suppose it to be.

that which, known to us only by its external attributes and not by its inner essence, we term matter.

Yet this Material Aspect of evolution is incomplete, and indeed incomprehensible, except in the light of its Conscious Aspect. This brings us to the direct consideration of those High Intelligences from whom proceed the wisdom to plan and the energy to stamp that original impress upon the plastic " root of matter" which remains an indelible and unalterable law for it throughout all its subsequent transformations and evolutionary processes. Here we approach the real problem; and here, in common with all religious and philosophical systems, we have to postulate a Causeless Cause, Omnipresent and Eternal, and having the Substance, Force, and Conscious Aspects to which reference has already been had, and upon the correlations and permutations of which all evolution depends. The late Subba Row, in his lectures on the Bhagavad Gita, regarding this Absolute, Causeless Cause, writes:

"Even the so-called atheists have never denied it. Various creeds have adopted various theories as to the nature of this Causeless Cause.* All sectarian disputes have arisen not from a difference of opinion as to its existence, but from the difference of the attributes which man's intellect has constantly tried to impose upon it. Is it possible to know anything about the Causeless Cause ? No doubt it is possible to know something about it. It is possible to know all about its manifestations, though it is next to impossible for

---

*The learned lecturer termed this throughout the First Cause, but as he evidently meant that which Theosophy, following the Secret Doctrine, recognizes as the Causeless Cause, reserving the term First Cause for the creative energy in manvantaric activity, I have accordingly taken the liberty to change the original reading in accordance with this, to avoid unnecessary confusion.

human knowledge to penetrate into its inmost essence, and say what it really is in itself. We know that it is subject to periods of activity and passivity. When cosmic pralaya comes, it is inactive; and when evolution commences, it becomes active. But even the real reason for this activity and passivity is unintelligible to our minds.

"This Causeless Cause, or Parabrahmam of the Vedantin philosophers, is not matter nor anything like matter. It is not even consciousness, because all we know of consciousness is with reference to a definite organism. What consciousness is or will be when separated from a vehicle in which to function is a thing utterly inconceivable to us, and not only to us but to any other intelligence which has the notion of self or Ego in it, or which has a distinct, individualized existence.

"Of course, every entity in this Cosmos must come under the head of Ego, Non-Ego, or Consciousness. But Parabrahmam, the Causeless Cause, does not come under any one of them. Nevertheless, it seems to be the One source of which Ego, Non-Ego, and Consciousness are manifestations, or modes of existence. In the case of every objective consciousness, we know that what we call matter, or Non-Ego, is, after all, a mere bundle of attributes. But whether we arrive at our conclusion by logical inference, or whether we derive it from innate consciousness, we always suppose that there is an entity—the real essence of the thing upon which all these attributes are placed—which bears these attributes as it were, the essence itself being unknown to us.

"Now this Parabrahmam, or Causeless Cause, which exists before all things in the Cosmos, is the one essence from which starts into existence a center of energy called the Logos. In almost every doctrine is formulated the existence of a center of spiritual energy which is unborn and eternal, and which exists in a latent condition in the bosom of the Causeless Cause at the time of pralaya, and starts as a center of conscious energy at the time of Cosmic activity. It is the first Ego in the Cosmos, and every other Ego and every other self is but its reflection or manifestation. It is the great mystery in the Cosmos, with reference to which all the initiations and all the systems of philosophy have been devised. It is not material nor physical in its constitution, and it is not objective; it is not different in substance as it were, or in essence, from the Causeless Cause, and yet at the same time it is different from it in having an individualized existence. It exists in a latent condition in the Causeless Cause at the time of pralaya, just as the sense of Égo, or 'I am I,' is latent in man during sleep.

"It must not be supposed that this Logos is but a single center of energy which is manifested by Parabrahmam, or the Causeless Cause. There are innumerable others. Their number is almost infinite. This first manifestation of Parabrahmam appears to it as Mulaprakriti."

That is to say, that the first conscious Beings in the Universe awaken to self-consciousness to find themselves in material forms or vehicles, precisely as we awaken to consciousness to find ourselves encased in these physical bodies. We know that our "I" is not the same as the matter which clothes it; similarly, the Logoi know that the "root" of matter which clothes them is only a clothing, and what the real nature and essence of that Causeless Cause, which calls into objective existence both the "I" of the Logoi and their material base, is as unknowable to the great and primal Ideation expressed in those First Logoi as is the source of our "I" and its physical vehicle to us.

At the first dawn of differentiation and consequent evolution matter has impressed upon it, from these First Logoi, the primal manifestation of Consciousness in the Cosmos—that impulse and directing energy which will carry it through all the successive and myriad phases of its succeeding evolutionary manifestations, to the time when the Great Pralaya, or Rest, shall interpose another period of inactivity, as certainly as that Niagara will carry over its sublime cataracts all the water which flows into

it from the great lakes. Remember, there is no evolution
of consciousness; but only an evolution of matter into
forms fitted to express higher and higher states or reflections of that Absolute Consciousness, which it is just as absurd and unscientific to predicate any additions to
through evolution, or in any other manner, as it' is to assume the "creation" of new matter. The matter of the
Universe is a whole, which can not be added to nor taken
from; Consciousness is also a whole, alike incapable of addition to or subtraction from.\ The relation of the one to
the other is, as already pointed out, all that falls under the
law of evolution; the real essence of both remains forever
untouched, resting in the bosom of the Causeless Cause.
This does not bar from our consideration intelligent supervision over the evolutionary impulse by those high,
Creative Logoi above referred to. For the whole scheme
of evolution, so far as it seems comprehensible to finite
beings, consists in and has for its motive the changing of
the relations between matter, force, and consciousness, so
that through this change undifferentiated consciousness
shall "evolve" into self-consciousness. It is only necessary that these Creative Beings should act in conformity
to those few primal and underlying laws which apparently
limit the Absolute itself, of which the law of cycles, the
law of karma, and the law of infinite Unity rendered manifest by infinite diversity, or variation, are examples. The
"I" in a man can and does take control of his body, for
instance, and transport it wheresoever it pleases, so long
as it acts in accordance with the underlying and basic laws
of mechanics and gravitation pertaining to this plane.
Man can, also, take matter and transform it into any
shape, or transport it to any place, if he keep within the

same bounds, or his possible as distinguished from his impossible. In like manner, these First Great Logoi can fashion worlds and even sentient beings in any manner they see fitting, so long as they, in turn, do not attempt to transcend their impossible, or those Absolute limitations pointed out above. And this working in harmony with and under the direction of this original impress of the First Logoi by intelligent, sentient, yet relatively lower beings, representing of necessity infinite degrees and grades of intelligence, is the true source of that much-harped-on "Design" which Christians assume as indubitable evidence of the existence of their personal Jehovah. Much of this creative, or fashioning, intelligence is evidently very greatly inferior to that of man in some aspects, though immensely transcending his powers in others. For instance, the intelligence which fashions the beautiful form and flowers of an apple-tree is not sufficient to prevent the seed which chances to fall under the angle of a stone wall from the hopeless task of attempting to penetrate this obstacle; nor even in the case of man's physical form—which is not created by the same order of intelligences that are the source of his intellect—will it suffice to stay the progress of an intended evolution of a human body, although this has been rendered plainly impossible by some intra-uterine accident or influence. This is the real source of the monstrosities in nature, which puzzle alike the scientist and theologian.

 If, now, we symbolize the Conscious-Aspect of the Absolute by physical light, then matter may be likened to a prism which decomposes it into many differing strata. Being thus decomposed, that which during pralaya was Absolute Unity, in manvantara manifests differing rates of conscious vibration, so to speak, just as the white light of the sun when passed through a prism is broken up into the varied colors of the spectrum, each having an entirely different rate of vibratory motion and wave length. Bearing in mind, then, that the One Consciousness, or One Life, is limited in its manifestations by the particular form of matter in which it is functioning, as the human vision is dark, clear, or colored, according to the physical media through which it attempts to look; and, further, that this matter itself is the result of differing rates of vibration acting upon and in the eternal Substance-Aspect of the Absolute—we get at least one turn of the key which at the seventh revolution shall unlock the secrets of evolution and objective life. We can perceive how these original cosmic curds, driven before the descending vibrations, the mechanical agents of evolution, assume coarser and more compact states as they touch successively lower vibrations of the Force-Aspect of the Causeless Cause. Having reached the lowest point in that which we ignorantly term "dead" or inorganic matter, under the stress of the original impulse they begin to ascend the evolutionary arc—to respond to successively finer and more delicate vibrations—thus affording ever clearer and more perfect forms, in which higher centers of consciousness can find suitable vehicles. 'At the beginning of manvantaric manifestation, it is the One life, represented in self-consciousness by the Logoi, or cosmic centers. When the impulse reaches our plane of matter, it is still the One life, but represented in self-consciousness here by the individualized centers of humanity.

The state of matter upon our little earth does not imply that all that in the solar system—much less the Cosmos—

is in similar conditions. Therefore, Consciousness is in as many various stages of expression as its material vehicle is in stages of evolution. From this it will be seen how necessary is the inference that there are infinite grades of intelligences both above and below us, as the result of the completed evolutions of other worlds, other systems, and even other manvantaras. A Logos, the first " I," which appears in the Cosmos at the manvantaric dawn, is an individualized center of self-consciousness which had attained to this stage at the close of the last great manvantara. With other Logoi, it becomes a duty to watch over and direct the successive evolutions which occur during the manvantara over which they thus preside. Below them are the various Hierarchies, Builders, Regents, Cosmoscratores, at work in the myriad departments of manifested nature.

The knowledge that one manvantara is the reincarnation of the entire Universe, having its karma, or causes, set up in preceding manvantaras, exactly corresponding to the reincarnation of the human soul, on its lower plane of operation, enables us to understand much that occurs. The Logoi would correspond to man's self-conscious, reincarnating Ego; these lower Hierarchies, Forces and Builders, to the universal "skandas," or forces which necessarily pass into latency at the striking of Universal pralaya. No manvantara can ever complete conscious evolution; and each must take up its work just as the human soul does—at the point it had attained when the universal dissolution of the Great Pralaya compelled its cessation. When the "hour" strikes for this universal pralaya, the consciousness ensouled in the lowest mineral bodies will first of all pass into a condition of latency, or that of bare

subjective potentiality of manifestation when fitting matter is again projected at another manvantaric dawn. This
enforced latency will be because the matter or combination of molecules it requires for its outer manifestation no
longer exists in the Universe, on account of the withdraw-
ing of the energy which caused it to appear. In like manner, will plane after plane of consciousness be reached, and
its entities, deprived of material form, be compelled to sleep
during the great eternity of unconsciousness which must
precede another reawakening of the Cosmos. All conscious beings, whether of high or low degree, will thus be
indrawn into the Absolute; yet while the consciousness of
lower forms remains only a potentiality, like that of a
sleeping or entranced man, to be again awakened at the
new Dawn, that of the highest ones will, we are told, pass
self-consciously into this great subjective arc of the cycle
of Eternal Duration. These are They, the Logoi, the
"luminous Sons of Manvantaric Dawn," who first awaken
to self-conscious life upon the objective plane at the new
manvantaric projection. Like our Higher Egos, which
represent the wisdom resulting from the sum of our
personal experiences, they represent the sum of manvantaric experience, and know that which has been and that
which is to be. They project the ideal plan of the manvantara that is to be through Their Divine Ideation, just
as an architect creates in his mind the plan of the magnificent structure, which may not be materialized except
by years of slow and tedious labor. Having this conception of what is to be, They may be said to have fore-
knowledge of it; but it is similar to the foreknowledge of
the architect of the structure he proposes to erect. This
ideal plan, first clothed with the divine Substance-Aspect

of the Absolute, stands as the eternal prototype of that which is to be, throughout its entire cycle. It is past, present, and future combined in an eternal Now. As it clothes and materializes itself by descending to successively lower and more material planes, we name the slow process, the successive stages of this unfolding, Time, and imagine that it marks real divisions of eternity. Could we approach nearer to the heart of Being this phantasmagoria of fleeting illusion would cease, and the time-harassed soul pass into eternal peace.

At each successive stage of this unfolding in time of the Divine Ideation, the entities, overtaken by the last pralaya, awaken from their long repose. They have no conception of the unthinkable periods which have passed them by, because they have not passed them by—time has not existed for them. Like the Seven Sleepers of Ephesus, their awakening finds them with no knowledge of any interval. The monad ensouled in the mineral atoms again reclothes itself as this form of matter appears, and the various Hierarchies, Cosmocratores and Builders resume their labors. The great workshop of nature, so long stilled, is again filled with its countless entities, each performing its proper office; making what progress it may, until the striking of another pralaya calls to another season of subjective being and rest. There are thus myriads of "Gods," or Creative Forces, or entities, in nature.

These different Orders of Creators or Builders must be accepted, if evolution is to be intelligently comprehended. It is as though the great Prism to which we have likened matter was capable of being acted upon by eternal Force or Motion until it gradually became more and more transparent and permitted higher and higher rates of vibrations of consciousness to pass through it. Thus, at the stage of "dead" matter the prism is so dense as only to permit the red rays or vibrations, so to speak, to pass.

Keeping to our simile, in these red rays there can only find expression that form of consciousness which is so different from the human that we call its matter "dead." Yet the impulse received at the manvantaric or creative dawn will not permit matter to rest in this or any other condition. So, very gradually, and requiring ages of geologic time, "dead" matter is lifted or forced up, until, like a mountain top at sunrise, it catches here and there the streams of the next color, or the orange vibrations; and, a higher consciousness being now permitted to obtain a foothold, the vegetable kingdom appears. Becoming, under the constant impact of the eternal motion, still more translucent, it transmits now the yellow rays, and animal consciousness makes its appearance upon the earth. Becoming still more refined, green rays are transmitted, and human consciousness is enabled to find a fitting vehicle and man appears upon the scene. And when matter has evolved to that state in which the remaining colors of the spectrum are permitted to pass, and a corresponding consciousness to function, who can even imagine its glorious potentialities!

CHAPTER IV.

THE INDIVIDUALIZATION OF THE SOUL.

CONSIDERING Consciousness, then, as an essential
aspect of the Causeless Cause, we have to postulate it as inhering potentially in every stratum or possible subdivision of the Substance-Aspect of the same
Causeless Cause, and as becoming a potency only by
virtue of this association. In like manner, matter may be
said to be a potentiality in all spirit or consciousness, and
as also becoming potent (evolving form) only by and
because of this association. As neither can manifest
upon the finite plane without the aid of the other, it is
useless to speculate as to their relative superiority. Because the consciousness which we recognize as self-consciousness in our thinking, feeling and willing Ego is evidently very greatly superior in function to the material
form or body with which it is associated, it does not follow that on their own plane the matter and consciousness
of the cells out of which this body is constructed are in
any similar degree of relative superiority and inferiority,
nor that the material basis in which our Ego has its own
proper habitation is in a relatively inferior state. Our
Egos, as will presently be shown, are now using these
bodies to bring themselves into sense relations with the
material plane, similarly as a scientist uses the microscope
to open up avenues of knowledge otherwise unattainable.
Matter of some degree is the great register upon which

the Conscious-Aspect of the Causeless Cause records its experiences. Without this association, continuity of conscious experiences could not be assured—unless we assume consciousness without any material basis whatever to be a possibility in nature, which position must always remain an assumption because unverifiable, unthinkable, and analogically unwarrantable from all phenomena to which we have present access. The immortality of that conscious center we recognize as our "I am myself" depends entirely, from its material aspect, upon the relative permanency or impermanency of the material tablets upon which it records its conscious experiences. And the "Primordial Substance" of Western philosophy, as well as the "mulaprakriti," or "root of matter," of the Eastern Vedantins—the Substance-Aspect of this study— is but the great and eternal tablet upon which Infinite Consciousness inscribes its finite experiences.

If, then, at the dawn of a new awakening to material existence, we have the re-emerging, in obedience to the law of cyclic activity, of consciousness clothed in material form, we may picture such consciousness as a bare potency only. It IS, but it can not be said to have any other attributes. It has clothed itself with appropriate Substance, under another great law of the Absolute unto itself—that of Cause and Effect. Passing by, for the present, those infinite variations of appropriate form resulting from the degrees of becoming attained by differing entities during past manvantaras, let us take up that which we may term monadic or (to us) undifferentiated consciousness. It represents as nearly as we can imagine pure, subjective potentiality of becoming. Yet in this first clothing of itself in its counterpart—pure, unimpressed,

virgin substance—it has imposed upon itself a limitation.
It has acquired the widening of consciousness resulting
from this association, and can never again return to its former condition of bare subjectivity.   Let us suppose that
this association, which for want of a better we may term
elemental, continues for a manvantara.   At that period, if
no sooner, the bond would be dissolved and the consciousness freed, to take a new clothing and attain a farther experience at the next great awakening of the Cosmos.
This time it can not re-enter just the same class or degree
of substance it did before, for it has something added to
it which makes it greater than before this addition.
Therefore, it must, under the stress of that which we term
natural evolution, seek higher avenues, and this plainly
and simply because of the mathematical axiom that the
lesser can not contain the greater.   It seeks, then, a
higher expression, and clothes itself, let us say, with that
which we know as mineral, or inorganic, matter.   It remains another planetary or minor manvantara in this
form until freed by another planetary or minor pralaya.

Under the same law it can not at a new world-birth reclothe itself in mineral matter; it must seek the vegetable
kingdom.   Thence it must pass to the animal, and from
thence be pushed to the human; and all this under the
necessity of natural law governing evolution of form, this
"natural law" being that primal impress upon it by the
Logoi at the great manvantaric dawn.

This is a general view of the process from its purely material aspect.   It of necessity only pictures half the reality, as all one-sided views must. ' There is also a conscious aspect, which must not be left out of consideration.
Retracing our steps to pick this up, let us pause to reflect

upon what must take place when bare, subjective consciousness has been released from its first association with a material vestment. We have seen, under the law that the lesser can not contain the greater, that it can not reclothe itself with the same undifferentiated matter again. Where, then, will it find material for its next and higher expression? Evidently, it can only do this by creating for itself vestments out of matter already the seat of consciousness in its own former and lower expression. So, if this lower expression be pictured in some inconceivable way as transcendentally atomic using this term "atom" in its ordinary scientific acceptation,—then it must synthesize and collect these transcendental atoms into, let us suppose, transcendental molecules, and of these build its higher habitation. By so doing it not only does not interfere with the evolution of form and the becoming in consciousness going on in these primitive atoms, but also actually aids and hastens this process by its own presence, and consequent imparting, to a degree at least, its own essence to this atomic consciousness with which it is thus, as it were, molecularly associated. This lifting up of lower consciousness by the presence and surrounding of higher is the spiritual aspect of the great evolutionary process, and one which the scientist resolutely refuses to recognize, although obeying its commands in his association with, and impress imparted to, the cells of his body every moment of his life. It has been called the Divine Law of Compassion, and an attribute of the very Absolute itself. Thus it is that the higher must help the lower; unconsciously in the lower kindoms, consciously in the higher—or try to oppose the highest law in nature, and perish! In this fact lies the oft-repeated assertion of

Theosophists that altruism is the law, and the only means of progress, upon the higher human planes at least. For man has become a self-conscious factor in that great scheme of evolution which has for its basis Divine compassion.

Recognizing, then, the dual aspect of that which we term evolution, but which is only an evolution of form and a becoming in consciousness, let us once more retrace our steps somewhat in our study of the becoming of the human soul. Yet in all this we must not lose sight of the fact that "every entity in the Universe either is, was, or prepares to become, a man."* We must not view man for one instant as apart from nature as a whole, or as not subject to her every law in common with all other entities whether of high or low degree. We have seen, in a general way, how the process of evolution, which has been well termed the Cycle of Necessity, forces entities into progressively higher forms of matter; that, in fact, every descent or involution of spirit, or consciousness, in matter is the exact equivalent of an evolution of material form. For the new descent compels the building of higher forms to contain, or to allow expression for, the entities crowded out—if the term be allowable—of their old habitations by the incoming guests. We have seen, also, that consciousness is at first monadic—using this term in its true sense of One-ness, and which is quite different from that in which we speak of the human Monad—and is only very gradually impressed with the stamp of any individual experience. It might be likened to the crude gold nuggets, which are simply gold at first, and indistinguishable from other nuggets until they become coins of different values

*Secret Doctrine.

under the various individualizing processes and stamps received in the mint.   If, now, we remember that this which we have termed a Great Manvantara, or objective arc of the Universe, is interrupted by an almost infinite number of minor pralayas, or subjective cycles of rest, of equally infinite degrees of incompleteness, we shall at length be in a position to appreciate evolution as we perceive its action in nature about us.   For under the general view, with which this chapter was prefaced, it would seem to have been inferred that only Great Pralayas, or times of Universal Rest, allowed of the liberation of consciousness and its consequent progression in future manvantaras.   This is By no means the case.   These pralayas extend from the unthinkable periods contemplated by the Brahmanical classification, and represented arithmetically by fifteen places of figures, to periods of perhaps less than a second, as in the case of the death and renewals of the molecules composing the cells of our bodies.   The death of a human body is only a pralaya or rest for the soul, affording another opportunity, after this rest is over, for further conscious experiences.   The death of a planet is its pralaya; and so on for· a cell, a sun, or any entity whatever.   These minor pralayas by no means restore consciousness to its absolute condition, as the Great Pralayas do, but only to relative and infinitely varying states of freedom from material form.   Thus, sleep is a pralaya which temporarily frees man's higher principles, while death is similar, but of much higher degree.   After the first, consciousness must return to the same body; after the second, it clothes itself with an entirely new one. Minor and incomplete pralayas, such as sleep, are often spoken of as Obscurations.

Returning from this necessary digression : The consciousness expressed in mineral form, upon its dissociation from any cause from this, could easily re-enter any, or
almost any, portion of the entire mineral kingdom.   So
the lowly forms of vegetable or animal life, respectively,
might easily be capable of a wide range of choice among
other lowly forms of their kingdoms.   But how about that
consciousness expressed in the elephant, the tiger, or the
stately tree, even?   Is it possible to conceive of a magnificent oak, for example, upon the destruction of its cellular clothing, re-entering a fungus or a daisy? or of the
carnivorous, cruel tiger reappearing as a dove?   These
would be but senseless attempts to make the lesser contain the greater; to pour the ocean into the thimble.

It is easy to see that each conscious experience added
makes it more and more difficult, as the ages go by, for a
reincarnating entity to even re-enter its own class; and
that thus, in its minor degree, it will travel its own cycle of
necessity, first as an element, then as a mineral, then a
plant, an animal, a man and—a god !   It is also comprehensible, if but dimly, how the beginnings of individuality
are thus faintly impressed upon potential centers of consciousness in kingdoms far below the human, or even the
animal.   How these potential centers themselves originate
is not a subject for finite inquiry; it is a mystery pertaining to the Great Unknowable Causeless Cause.   We
only know that they do originate; and, as stated, may,
without transcending finite limits, dimly conceive of their
after processes.   It is within our power, also, to imagine
—and even to trace—a pathway by following which we
can perceive that, after unthinkable periods of conscious
experiences in lower forms, there would at last come a

time when a conscious center forced into a higher kingdom would recognize that this state was unlike former
ones—and, lo! the mystery of self-consciousness is
achieved, and a human soul has become! For self-consciousness is but the recognition that our consciousness is
different from that of entities around us, the differentiation of Ego from Non-Ego. This once recognized, all
our magnificent introspective or subjective mental processes become only a question of widening phenomenal
experience.

Yet the view of man's becoming will still be one-sided
if we lose sight of the spiritual aspect of evolution, already
referred to. Every advanced entity in the Universe, as
we have seen, is forced during the Cycle of Necessity, by
this grand law of involution, *plus evolution*, to clothe itself
with entities occupying lower forms of matter. It thus
secures its own continued conscious experiences, and mer-
cifully assists those with which it is thus associated to rise
in the scale of being. This is the true mystery of man's
relation to the bodies in which he is incarnated. He is
using lower forms of life to enable him to obtain conscious
experiences on the material plane. Until this simple explanation is recognized by Western nations they will continue to grope between the Scylla of materialistic nega-
tion and Charybdis of dogmatic superstition.

Once this spiritual aspect of evolution is recognized,
however, much of the mystery of man's dual nature, of
those two souls which Gœthe declares strive in every
human breast, becomes intelligible. The entities—our
Higher Egos—thus occupying the highly complex molecular associations composing our bodies, light up, by their
presence in this form, a reflection of the pure flame con-

stituting their own higher essence. Having thus rationalized that which was before but physical senses common to all animals as well as animal man, they—or we—can now relate themselves to this plane of phenomena through this reflection thus imparted by their presence. But, alas, in rationalizing they have not destroyed the desires and passions of purely animal, sensuous existence. On the contrary, these are strengthened a thousand-fold by being thus illumined by reason. There has been added to the sensuous delight that of anticipation as well as remembrance. The reasoning, remembering animal now runs riot in its mad chase after sensuous delights. And to control this fatally beautiful animal, to spiritualize senses thus rationalized, is the hard task set before every human soul. This is the conflict—the two souls within our breast fighting for mastery—which has been the theme of many an inspired poem, from the Bhagavad Gita down to the humble Salvation Army enthusiast who sings, " My Soul, be on thy guard!" Yet this very conflict strengthens, even as the fierce winds only cause the oak to strike more deeply its roots into the earth. It is a necessary part of the great scheme of evolution—a rugged, dangerous portion of that way which " leads up hill to the very end."

CHAPTER V.

REINCARNATION — PHILOSOPHIC AND LOGICAL EVIDENCE.

THE preceding chapters having, it is believed, established the fact that man has a center of consciousness, or soul, quite independent of the body for its existence, or conscious functions—except as the sense organs of the latter relate it to the material plane of the Cosmos, —those remaining will be devoted to a study of the nature of the relations sustained by this soul to the body. Standing first and foremost among these is the fact of its reincarnation, or its successive occupation of many bodies during its evolution through matter.

Reincarnation is quite distinct from metempsychosis, when this is understood to mean the return of the soul to earth through human or animal bodies indifferently; for it emphatically denies that, having once attained the human state, the soul can ever retrograde into an animal condition. A human soul has developed, as we have seen in the study of its evolution, certain qualities and potencies which are as incapable of functioning in an animal body as the tissues of a giant oak are incapable of being mechanically recompressed within the limits of the original acorn out of which it grew.

A correct conception of Reincarnation recognizes that the body, as such, has no part in the soul's return to earth; that the connection of the body with the soul is, primarily, to furnish sense organs to relate the latter to a plane so far beneath its own spiritual nature as to be reached only by this means; and, secondarily, in the matter of which the body, or bundle of sense organs, is constructed reside certain "qualities" the nature of which it is essential to the intellectual progress of the soul that it learn. For it is only by experiencing its "opposite" that true knowledge of any "quality" in nature, whether physical, mental or spiritual, can be obtained. Matter upon the fourth plane of any world is said to be "kamic," or full of "*rajas*," or desire. Hence, anger, passion, malice, envy, ambition, and a host of similar "qualities" of matter, are brought directly to the cognizance of the soul by means of its incarnating in a body full of them. Out of the experience of these, so undergone, it acquires a knowledge of the true nature of their opposites; and evolves a wisdom it could never gather but for this association with a body. This will be more fully explained in the chapter upon the Reincarnating Ego.

To Western minds, Reincarnation is both unfamiliar and distasteful. The unfamiliarity is due, perhaps, to the materialistic tendencies of its great thinkers, especially in the domain of science. Most scientists have been, and are, unwilling to admit the existence of a soul in man, to say nothing of its reincarnating.

That the idea should be distasteful to the unphilosophic mind, especially if trained to base all concepts, whether human or divine, upon personality and separateness, is not surprising. The superstructure of modern civilization is erected upon a foundation of individualism, and this in its lowest and most material sense. To succeed in life is its one object, and by success is understood the acquirement of wealth or fame. The view which involves a suc-

cession of lives in its perspective is necessarily lost sight
of with horizons rigidly defined by matter. "When we
are dead it is for a long time," a remark by a French
cynic, fairly presents the conception of life from the modern materialistic and utilitarian standpoint. That he who
does not make the most of it is missing opportunities
which will never again offer, is generally accepted. From
this it necessarily follows that strong personalities should
evolve as the soul returns, life after life, with its longing
for riches, fame, or power strengthened and confirmed by
successive partial realizations. Therefore, when Western
people are told that death ends the career of Mr. Smith,
who has amassed millions, or of Mr. Brown, who has become a great general, and that all that really survives in
any life are certain higher, spiritual thoughts and aspirations which have become foreign to the very motive of
our Western civilization, they are naturally repulsed.
The Christian heaven, with its guarantee of the eternal
persistence of the entire Mr. Smith, minus his body but
plus a pair of wings, seems much more desirable.

But that Reincarnation should be unsatisfactory to the
philosophic mind is unaccountable. For materialistic philosophy deliberately parts with life at the death of the
body; and in view of the utter blank beyond the grave—
the terrible, awful conception of ceasing to be—it would
seem reasonable that it should seize eagerly upon any ten-
able hypothesis which promises an extension of being.
Yet, of all classes, materialists are the most eager to prove
that when the curtain falls at death the play is over, except to new audiences.

The proofs of the Reincarnation of the soul follow, logically, as a corollary to the evidence of its existence as an

entity independent of the body; for a soul shown to
possess powers superior to its tenement must have brought
such faculties and powers with it, and will necessarily take
them when it departs.   The only remaining evidence
required, then, is to connect the source of this superiority with Reincarnation in successive bodies, such as,
or similar to, those we now possess.   This evidence may
be conveniently studied under its logical, or philosophical
and scientific aspects.

Taking up, primarily then, the logical and philosophic
portion of our enquiry, it may be said that there are three
hypotheses concerning the origin and destiny of the soul,
under which almost every possible form of belief may be
classified.   The first, and that which is held by a very
large majority of the human race, is Reincarnation, or the
repeated descent of the soul into material bodies.   The
second is the one-birth theory, which supposes the creation of a new soul at each birth, and having its chief rep-
resentative in modern—not ancient—Christianity.   It
also includes most of the believers in Spiritualism.   The
third looks upon the soul as the product of the molecular
and chemical activities going on within the body, and
holds that the cessation of these activities necessitates its
destruction.   This is the theory of modern materialism.
Now, if we apply the crucial test of an hypothesis—that
of accounting for all the phenomena included within its
own proper territory—we shall be at once in a position to
judge of the truth or falsity of each of these three concerning the soul.

First, then, as to the object of life.   Except we deny
any aim at all in Nature's processes which have led up to
man, it is evident that in man the one paramount object is

to gain knowledge and wisdom through experience. Even one short life forces us to this conclusion. Materialism does not deny this, but claims that this increment of wisdom is transmitted to the race, and that the individual has no future share in it. If experience and wisdom resulting therefrom be the object, then one life is simply absurd. Did all attain old age, the case would be bad enough, but when we consider the vast number who die with no experience whatever, the inadequacy of one life to accomplish this purpose becomes apparent to the dullest intellect.

As has been well shown by a recent writer:*

"The usual belief is that we are here but once, and once for all determine our future. And yet it is abundantly clear that one life, even if prolonged, is no more adequate to gain knowledge, acquire experience, solidify principle, and form character, than would one day in infancy be adequate to fit for the duties of mature manhood. Any man can make this even clearer by estimating, on the one hand, the probable future which Nature contemplates for humanity, and, on the other, his present preparation for it. That future includes evidently two things—an elevation of the individual to god-like excellence, and his gradual apprehension of the Universe of Truth. His present preparation, therefore, consists of a very imperfect knowledge of a very small department of one form of existence, and that mainly gained through the partial use of misleading senses; of a suspicion, rather than a belief, that the sphere of super-sensuous truth may exceed the sensuous as the universe does this earth; of a partially developed set of moral and spiritual faculties, none acute and none unhampered, but all dwarfed by non-use, poisoned by prejudice, and perverted by ignorance; the whole nature, moreover, being limited in its interests and affected in its endeavor by the ever-present needs of a physical body which, much more than the soul, is felt to be the

*The Necessity for Reincarnation.   Leaflet.

real 'I.' Is such a being, narrow, biased, carnal, sickly, fitted to enter at death on a limitless career of spiritual acquisition ?

"Now, there are only three ways in which this obvious unfitness may be overcome,—a transforming power in death, a post-mortem and wholly spiritual discipline, a series of Reincarnations. There is nothing in the mere separation of soul from body to confer wisdom, ennoble character, or cancel dispositions acquired through fleshliness. If any such power resided in death, all souls, upon being disembodied, would be precisely alike,—a palpable absurdity. Nor could a post-mortem discipline meet the requirement, and this for the following reasons : (*a*) the soul's knowledge of human life would always remain insignificant; (*b*) of the various faculties only to be developed during incarnation, some would still be dormant at death, and therefore never evolve ; (*c*) the unsatisfying nature of material life would not have been fully demonstrated; (*d*) there would have been no deliberate conquest of the flesh by the spirit; (*e*) the meaning of Universal Brotherhood would have been very imperfectly seen ; (*f*) desire for a career on earth under different conditions would persistently check the disciplinary process; (*g*) exact justice could hardly be secured ; (*h*) the discipline itself would be insufficiently varied and copious; (*i*) there would be no advance in the successive races on earth.

"There remains, then, the last alternative, a series of Reincarnations, or, in other words, that the enduring principle of the man, endowed during each interval between two earth-lives with the results achieved in the former of them, shall return for further experience and effort."

The author then proceeds to show how all of the objections are met and fully satisfied through Reincarnation; thus :

"Only through Reincarnation can knowledge of human life be made exhaustive, or opportunity afforded for the development of all those faculties which can only be developed during incarnation. Only through reincarnations is the unsatisfying nature of material life fully demonstrated; the subordination of the lower to the higher nature made possible; the meaning of Universal Brotherhood become apparent; the desire for other forms of earthly experience be extinguished by undergoing them; exact justice meted to every man; variety and copiousness to the discipline we all require, be secured; and a continuous advance in the successive races of men ensured."

Justice, especially, is most completely set aside by any other theory. According to Christian dogmas, a child who dies at birth is surely "saved." It has had none of the experience and temptations of its fellow-mortals, yet its future happiness is eternally assured because of the acci-. dental cutting short of its earthly career. A Christian who really believes this ought to pray for death for his children, and return devout thanks when the grave closes over their little forms. For what are the pleasures of one brief life compared with the eternal happiness which, according to their belief, awaits the child just beyond the grave, and which it runs the hazard of losing if its existence is prolonged sufficiently for it to encounter the many temptations which must await it in the event of its surviving? Nor is the Spiritist happier in his efforts to explain away the inconsistencies of one life. He claims that experience may be acquired by proxy in a spiritual realm. This postulates the absurdity of attaining material knowledge under spiritual environments. But were this possible, it still banishes both method and reason from the scheme of evolution, for there is either no necessity for the spirit to incarnate at all, or else the coming to earth for a few moments, as in the case of babes who die at birth, cannot fulfill the requirements. And this without speaking of the injustice of compelling one soul to undergo the pains of mortal experience in order that it may teach another to whom accident or disease denied opportunity.

Either this world is one of chance, "where Chaos umpire
sits, and by decision adds but to the confusion," or else all
one-birth theories must be set aside, as not accounting for
even a small portion of the observed facts.

The same fatal defects apply to the materalistic theory
of the non-existence of a soul independently of the body.
For admitting that experience and wisdom might be
transmitted to the race as its heritage, yet the race itself
must eventually perish, and with it all the fruits of the sufferings of its units.   Materialism merely removes the difficulty one step, and leaves life none the less a farce because this now assumes colossal proportions.   It is quite
as unjust for the race to die, even after millions of years,
as it is for the individual to do so after one life.   Both results argue the non-existence of any design in nature, and
relegate the whole problem of human life to either pure
chance, or else the barbarous whim of some Jehovah, who
creates and destroys men and worlds as the humor suits
him.   No sane man can deny the evidence of intelligent
design in nature.   His imperfect physical senses make
this plain, and the most powerful microscope or telescope
only adds to the evidence already at hand.   The more
deeply one searches the more abundant the proofs become.   This is admittedly the law of the physical plane.
Having reached the mental or spiritual plane, does nature
now suddenly fly in the face of her former methods and
hand the guiding reins over to blind fate or blinder
chance ?

Materialism is particularly unhappy, also, in applying its
negative hypothesis to its own grandest and most sweep-
ing generalizations.   It proudly announces that *ex nihilo
nihil fit*, and then assumes an intelligent, reasoning soul as

starting into existence "out of nothing," and departing into the same unreasonable and impossible limbo when certain processes pertaining to the bodily form cease to be active. The indestructibility of matter, the correlation of force, the conservation of energy, the law of evolution— all are in hopeless irreconcilability with the materialistic theory, as they also are to the one-birth hypothesis. Matter, force, and intelligence are, as has been pointed out, but three aspects of the One Reality, the CAUSE-LESS CAUSE, and their separation under any condition is absolutely unthinkable. If matter is indestructible, then the material base of the soul is indestructible; if force is always conserved, then this includes psychic or soul force; if energy is eternal in its action, then intellectual energy cannot be excluded; if evolution be a fact in nature, then it includes the larger fact that its processes are necessarily infinite in duration.

But materialism fancies it sees a loophole for avoiding these conclusions in the fact that matter, force, and energy reappear as things apparently differing from their former modes of manifestation. Granted; but these apparent differences are only the masks which the one actor assumes upon taking differing parts. It is the same actor, whose real identity is always one throughout the entire performance. It is not claimed by Theosophy that the soul functions in the same manner when using the sense organs of the body as it does when this limitation is no longer interposed. But it is always the soul, and nothing else, although its phenomena are necessarily modified by the form of matter with which it is temporarily associated. Heat and light are none the less one because differing conditions cause them to display differing modes of motion; and no mode of motion, which links the material aspect of nature to the spiritual, has ever been traced to a transmutation into any form of intelligence. The two are opposite facets of the ONE, and can never interchange on the plane of manifestation. It is for this reason that the soul must persist as intelligence; its force can only be conserved by that which is essentially itself in properties. Scientists claim that atoms of matter can never escape from the laws of affinity; that atoms of iron, for instance, will ever be attracted to iron atoms, and that no power can destroy that particular property which constitutes the atom iron, instead of, for example, gold, although it may be so buried among other atoms as to be entirely indistinguishable by our coarse physical senses. So intelligence must follow the same law, by all the evidence of analogy. The soul represents, in its " I am I" manifestation, an ultimate division—if we may be allowed the term—of intelligence, and must retain its " I am I" qualities under whatever associations it may find itself; just as truly, as reasonably, and as certainly as that the ultimate material atom whose properties constitute it iron can never be destroyed nor changed into something which is not iron. If the one is law on the material plane, the other is equally law on the psychic. The physical atom represents the unit of matter; the " I am I" represents the unit of consciousness. From both, the idea of magnitude or extension in space is excluded. Certainly, the " I am I" can not be conceived as limited by the size or any other physical qualities of any body with which it is associated. It is, as we have said, the unit of Consciousness—the true basis of all manifestations of intelligence in nature, as the atom is the unit of matter, and the physical basis of all material forms.

So with materialistic concepts of evolution. As we have pointed out, there is just as great a defect in logic, and as fatal a disagreement between the hypothesis and the fact that design pervades every department of nature, in annihilating a race, as there is in predicating the annihilation of the individual soul. If uncounted millions of individuals are to be sacrificed to perfect a glorious race only for this, too, to be ultimately annihilated, then the evil and unreason of creation are only magnified, not removed.

But once admit the fact of reincarnation, and observe how the apparent chaos of injustice changes into the most beautiful harmony. Apparently discordant and irreconcilable phenomena are marshaled into orderly array; confusion and injustice disappear, and life assumes a deeper and more significant meaning. The terrible inequalities of birth, utterly inexplicable by the single-birth, and still more so by the materialistic hypothesis, are shown to be the result of causes set in operation by the soul itself in former incarnations, and not the careless or stupid incapacity of some personal god playing at creation, and making a sad mess of it. The wretch born of drunken and vicious parents, amid such surroundings as make virtue practically a miracle, foredoomed to a life of want and woe, has created such attractions in former lives as render it impossible for him to be born under any other conditions. No cruel fate nor blind chance has been the slightest factor in bringing about the result. Just as surely as the magnet turns to the north, so surely will the helpless soul be drawn to those parents having the greatest sum of similar attractions. The acid poured freely into a vessel containing a solution of a hundred alkaline bases will with unerring certainty combine with that, and with that only, for which it has the greatest affinity. How much more surely, then, will the soul seek out its strongest affinities at the moment of reincarnation than the so-called unconscious atoms on a plane so far beneath it !

There is no other theory which will account for the infinite variations of character which appear from the very moment of birth. To say nothing of our material environments, to omit all notice of the manifest injustice which SENDS equally helpless souls to rich or poor, to civilized or cannibalistic, to black or white parents, or any of the other infinite variations of merely physical circumstances, we do not start fair in the race from a moral and intellectual standpoint. One child is born with genius, another an idiot—both of parents of about the same mental capacity, it may be. What cause brought about this great and unjust difference, if neither lived before? One infant comes into the world handicapped by a sullen temper and vicious disposition; another, with the most lovable traits. If it is claimed, as materialism erroneously asserts, that each inherits its peculiarities from its parents, even then how can reason accept the black injustice which sends one soul to the pure parents, and the other to the impure ones, if neither had had any previous voice in the matter? We must accept reincarnation if we would ever hope to solve the awful inequalities which attend upon birth. No man could find it in his heart to condemn his child to be born a poor, innocent victim of such fiendish caprices, such an unavoidable life of temptation, suffering, degradation and death, followed by an eternal hell, as birth to vicious, barbarous, or even ignorant parents almost surely presupposes; yet Christians believe this horrible thing of a Jehovah whom they claim to be of infinite compassion and mercy! It is the logical outcome, however, of a philosophy whose most learned divines calmly discuss with approval such topics as: " The Loving Kindness of God as Evidenced in the Eternal Punishment of Sinners!"* and "The Greatness of God as shown in the SLOW Christianizing of the Earth!"†

Again, as we have seen, the fact that no two individuals of the entire human race were ever born with the same character, or ever acquired the same, is one of the strongest logical proofs of the truth of reincarnation. Each babe comes into the world with the stamp of its former desires, appetites and experiences indelibly impressed upon it in the form of this individual character. Materialism claims ante-natal influence within the womb as the cause of this infinite divergence in human character; but the proof that this is not so is too abundant. Were there none other, the cases of twin births would suffice; for here the ante-natal influence must be absolutely the same, yet from the hour of birth twin infants often show the most marked differences in disposition and character. It is true that most twins, for obvious reasons—chief among which is the affinity which drew both to the same parents at the same time—display marked similarity in mental and physical characteristics; but a working hypothesis must be one which explains all the phenomena, and these occasional divergences completely nullify ante-natal influence as a factor.

---

*Irenics.   Jas. Strong, S. T. D., LL. D.
†A paper by a Minister in a Christian magazine.   Indexed in "The Review of Reviews."

The almost infinite differences in human character
have a most profound bearing upon any philosophy of life,
and can only be explained by admitting the fact of reincarnation; for the character as displayed by babes from
the moment of birth, and which throughout life separates
each man from all other men, is the sum of the experiences
the Ego, or soul, has already undergone and assimilated,
and which experiences remain as indelible impressions
upon and modifications of the soul's conscious area, and
constitute the differences which distinguish it from other
souls.   Had all souls similar experiences character would
be inconceivable, for all would be alike.

Much of the desires and passions which constitute the
larger portion of the soul's activities at any given time are
necessarily suspended by the change called death, and
therefore remain dormant, or latent, until it is compelled
by its karmic affinities to again seek incarnation, when
they become active with the opportunity afforded by a
new body.   Just as a man's passions are held in abeyance
by sleep, to regain all their former activity upon awakening, so all his desires and appetites which are so gross
and earthly as to lie below the planes of Devachan,* remain inoperative, but by no means destroyed, until he
again awakens to earth life in his new dwelling.   It is for
this reason that "character" is so important an element in
reincarnation.   It is simply the old affinities man has himself created acting upon all planes; determining the kind of
body in which he shall find his new habitation; the
family, the nation, the race, the social station, the intellectual trend, the predisposition to disease or long life,

*DEVACHAN—The subjective cycle intervening between two
earth lives.   See chapter on Post-mortem States.

and every other conceivable limitation in the environment or circumstances of the new life. All these limitations are effects resulting from causes set in operation in former lives, which causes have, under the law of Karma, or Cause and Effect, delivered his soul, a helpless, unconscious captive, to do with whatsoever this Supreme Law shall determine. For during the subjective, or devachanic, interim between earth lives the human will is in complete abeyance. It becomes a potency during earth life because man has acquired self-consciousness upon this plane—has, under that which Eastern philosophy terms the Great Heresy, separated Ego from Non-Ego, and in consequence of this delusion too often opposed his will to that of nature. Not so, in devachan. Here only the spiritual will is consciously functioning and all the unexpended material or sensuous causes generated in past earth lives, and especially in the last of these, exert their full affinities entirely below the present conscious plane of the Ego, and it only awakens from its devachanic existence to find itself in a body, which, under the karmic law of Cause and Effect, is thus, unconsciously to it, predetermined.

During one incarnation the thousands of thoughts, emotions, and mental states included in our every-day life, and constituting that thread or consciousness which materialism insists is all there is at the base of our "I am I," constantly crystallize into habits, desires, and instinctive tendencies to assume certain mental attitudes to the exclusion of others; all of which enters into the composition of our personal character. This latter, in its larger degree, is again crystallizing into our true or individual character, or that of our reincarnating Ego, or soul. The memory of

the myriad states of consciousness by which this permanent character is acquired is left behind at each death of
the body; but the result, the sum total, is carried over at
reincarnation to the new account.   The statue preserves
no record of the ten thousand strokes of the chisel by
which it was chipped into shape, yet the result is none the
less beautiful because of this.

〔Reincarnation, then, affords the key, and the only key,
to the mysteries of the inequalities of birth; for the great
divergence of character and mental capacity, ranging from
genius to idiocy, at birth, accounts for the presence of evil
in the world, explains "original sin," makes immortality
reasonable by extending the existence of the soul to an
infinite past as well as to an eternal future.   The last
point mentioned—existence in both directions—avoids the
absurdity of postulating a semp- or half-eternal being—an
existence with but one end, which a soul created at birth
and having immortality from that point presupposes.   A
line must have two ends, whether it be physical or
spiritual.

Reincarnation, also, is in perfect accord with the scientific conceptions of the persistence of force and the conservation of energy; and shows how a cause, once set in
motion, must have its effect; that energies generated in
one life cannot be cut short by death, but must find expression in a future one; that the affinity which guides a
soul into the most fitting body to express its characteristics is but an exemplification of the law of energy or
force taking the direction of the least resistance.

No effort is lost; soul force, like all other forms of force,
is ever conserved.   The soul which has longed and struggled for a desired result, finding its efforts cut short by

death when, perhaps, on the very point of realization, does not lose the fruit of its toil and self-denial. The energy so generated will accompany, guide, and control the next birth so as to continue its expression in one unbroken line. No effort, whether for good or evil, can be without its results. It is a cause, and in the eternal harmony of nature must have its corresponding effect.

CHAPTER VI.

REINCARNATION—THE SCIENTIFIC EVIDENCE.

BUT aside from all philosophic necessities or hypotheses, if Reincarnation be true, we shall find evidence of it in nature, for *natura non saltet.* At the outset of this portion of our inquiry, we see that the repetition of her processes is universal. In the mineral kingdom, the sand, formed from the crumbling rocks of the mountain's side, re-forms into stony stratifications, at the bottom of the sea, to be again upheaved, and reprint the geologic page in future ages. Tree or plant, animal or human, each is reproduced "after its kind," in an apparently endless succession. Embryologists trace the history of the incalculable periods during which the physical form of man evolved up through the lower kingdoms by means of the repetition of each successive stage, in gestation. Cell, fish, reptile, bird, animal, man—each step upward is repeated, though the necessity for this would seem to have ceased with the completion of the more perfect design. Man casts aside his 'prentice efforts once he succeeds, but nature ever follows the familiar pathways.

Yet the countless elemental hosts and hierarchies of "nature Spirits," engaged in carrying out the practical aspect of evolution do not pause at the simple reproduction of the old form. Having reached the end of beaten paths, each still struggles onward, though its progress is as little perceptible as the impress of a single wave upon the beach which, nevertheless, is slowly wearing away.

This gradual perfection of type also shows that idea precedes form, and that nature is not working blindly, under the impulse of unintelligent force. Ages were occupied in so modifying the gills of water-breathing mammalia that they could live in the purer, rarer atmosphere of the earth; yet is it not evident that the idea of the perfected bird was present and potent during the whole process? Is it not also evident that the idea of perfected man, with all his wonderful organization, was present when the first protoplasmic cell responded to the force of the inner, energizing thought?

It will be universally admitted that it is the idea, and not the form, which is preserved; the point of dispute is as to the method by which the idea is carried onward. The materialist avers that it is due to physical procreation alone; that, for instance, if the dove should become unfertile, the idea of it would perish off the earth with the cessation of its physical existence. The Theosophist denies this, and declares that if every dove on earth were to die nature is amply able to reproduce the form out of the pre-existing idea from whence it evolved the species. The materialist affirms that force and matter have, by the merest chance, brought about the evolution of form and intelligence; that both these are but properties of matter, and are dissipated with the dissolution of the chemical and vital forces which caused their manifestation. The Theosophist declares that spirit, or consciousness, underlies and is the basis of all form, and passes from form to form as these decay or become unfitted for its further occupation. As Plato declares, "The soul weaves ever her garments anew." To interrogate nature as to her methods of taking these subjective steps in pursuit of her objects constitutes the motive of this chapter.

Our first inquiry must be as to the identity of consciousness when passing from vehicle to vehicle. That is, does the same conscious entity ensoul successive bodies? From the human standpoint, the answer to this question is all important. To the kingdoms below man we look for the proof of the affirmative of the question, as under the law of evolution there must be a preparation for, or a beginning of, the processes necessary.

It would seem that every center of consciousness forming within the All-Consciousness, or Over Soul, retains its individuality under all circumstances, except two, which two are practically one. These are: (*a*) the failure to maintain itself in the struggle with nature's warring elements, and a consequent loss of identity as an entity; and, (*b*) the passing through and beyond the Cycle of Necessity, and returning laden with the spoils of conscious victories to the all-embracing Over Soul, which latter process involves no real loss of individual identity. Certainly, up to the point where consciousness is developed sufficiently to take control of its own destinies, there can hardly be any lapsing back predicated; for the original Energy which set the evolutionary forces in operation—the Outbreathing of the Great Breath—can not fail before this stage, because the force is practically omnipotent. And after this the will of the innumerable centers of developed consciousness represent and stand instead of that original Energy which can not be diminished, and of which they in their totality are the undiminished correlations. Yet, as on the material plane, certain laya centers—of worlds, even—may lose themselves by a succession of apposite unfavorable causes, so there can arise in the evolution of every soul destructive causes, set up by itself, which end in its annihilation as a self-conscious center of energy.

From these premises the inference is justified that an entity representing an apparent separation of consciousness, whether its outer physical clothing be a plant, a tree, an animal, or the human form, maintains its individuality throughout the major half, if not the whole, of the planetary cycle, or minor manvantara; that is, that the consciousness (elemental in this case) of a tree reincarnates or re-embodies itself in another tree; and similarly for all organisms throughout animated nature. For the monadic base, the Ray from the Causeless Cause, upon which all shades and grades of differentiated consciousness rest, must be absolutely colorless. It is only by material experience or expression that it gets this. But having once received a definite stamp in any kingdom, as was pointed out in the study of the Individualization of the Soul, it has acquired individuality to this extent, and individuality thus impressed upon it can not be removed. It may be added to, as when vegetable consciousness is added to mineral, and animal to this; but to remove it is unthinkable. Therefore, it logically follows that the consciousness of a tree or plant impressed upon a monadic base renders it impossible for this monadic center to again re-enter the mineral kingdom, just as the human consciousness, once attained, renders it impossible for the human soul to again reincarnate in an animal, or any lower form. It would be making the lesser contain the greater—a mathematical impossibility and logical absurdity. For this reason, consciousness, having reached any definite point of expression, can only remain stationary, in opposition to the evolutionary impulse, or go forward in harmony with this.

We have thus the strongest and most cogent reason for predicating the identity of any monadic expression of consciousness when passing from form to form, upon the disintegration or death of these. For the consciousness of a bear, for instance, to lapse back into a universal reservoir of conscious force, as taught by some materialistic hypotheses, implies the destruction of all those emotions and instincts which distinguish the character of the animal. Now, consciousness is only related to the material plane in terms of motion or force, and this is universally admitted to be indestructible. Then how is it possible to destroy that force which expresses animal instinct? It cannot be destroyed; it must find expression on the animal plane, and in the bear, or some closely allied species, until it is transmuted by evolution, and the consequent widening of its consciousness into higher forms of conscious expression.

There is, thus, an absolute and logical necessity for specific reincarnation, of plant in plant, animal in animal, and man in man, and it only remains to examine the methods which nature adopts to secure this end.

It is evident that the universal repetition of idea in form throughout all nature, to which we have called attention, is but the expression of a deep and basic law. This law is that all existence proceeds in cycles, each having its objective and its subjective arc. Eastern occult philosophy terms the action of this universal law the "Great Breath," a definition in which Theosophy coincides and adopts. That finite time is related to Infinite

Duration by means of these cycles of existence, is a great and all-embracing truth, without the proper recognition of which no intelligent conception of reincarnation can be formulated. From the major manvantara, occupying unthinkable eons of years, to the life of a single cell, lasting, in many instances, but a few moments, the rhythmic flow of motion and consciousness from without within, and from within without, is absolute, universal, without exception. Objective life succeeds subjective life, subjective life is followed by objective, in an eternal succession. The chain cannot be broken; it is as continuous as Duration itself.

In the vegetable kingdom, this ebb and flow of conscious force is within material limits largely, and easily studied. Especially in the annuals of cold or temperate climates is this flux and efflux plainly apparent. Every year a large portion of the material form dies down. All the beautiful imagery and design expressed in leaf, stalk, and flower perish as completely as though they had never existed. The life force has ebbed, yet not entirely. Root, rhizoma, or bulb hold in subjective embrace every detail, even to the most minute; and when the subjective cycle is completed the inner, subjective entity thrills, expands, clothes itself again with its vestment of cells, and reproduces the dead plant in all its former perfection and beauty. Every such a reproduction by a root or bulb is a genuine, specific reincarnation of the same elemental center of consciousness, or "elemental soul,"* in the same

---

*A "soul," or vehicle of consciousness [see Introduction], is termed "elemental" when below the plane of self-consciousness; "human," when it reaches this plane; "divine," when it passes it. Every entity in the Universe either "is, was, or prepares to become, a man."

plant, yet we fail to recognize this.   To us, nothing unusual has taken place—nor has there—because of our
familiarity with the phenomenon.   We say the plant has
"grown" again from the root.   But, in growing, it has followed a definite plan and idea.   Was this hidden in the
shriveled mass of matter, which gave no indication of its
presence whatever?   Doubtless; but how?   The form
was not hidden; only the elemental entity in its subjective
arc, or "pralaya," representing the "idea" of the plant.
In other words, the plant has been living a subjective life,
without losing one iota of that distinguishing character
which made it a denizen of a definite genus, family, and
species.   Because of the apparent clinging to material
form in root, bulb, or seed, the reality and importance of
the subjective arc of the existence of the plant entity has
been lost sight of.   There has not been that total separation of subjective from objective which we find upon
higher planes.   There has been a preparing for, an experiment in, subjective consciousness without entirely abandoning the material vestment, which is just what analogy
would have led us to expect in this kingdom, for *natura
non saltet.*

Indeed, it would seem reasonable to suppose that it is
only by clinging to some portion of the material form that
specific reproduction would be most practicable here; for
vegetable, like mineral, consciousness is so little differentiated, its monadic base so general and diffused, that a
total abandonment of the material form is to be expected
to prove the exception rather than the rule.   Where plants
are reproduced from the seed, in many seeds plainly, and
probably in all if we had the proper means of examination, the form of the plant to be reproduced is already

partially expressed in terms of matter. Witness the Hindu emblem of immortality, the lotus, and all cotyledonous plants. In fact, the essential part of any seed is the embryo, upon which one or more leaves are often capable of being distinguished. There is no doubt that nature-elementals can and do really incarnate any ideal form by starting from a single cell, and that any lost form could be so reproduced; but the inquiries undertaken in this chapter do not lie along this particular line. It is reincarnation we are studying—not incarnation in general terms.

This incomplete reincarnation is universal upon all planes, but of course is most marked in the comparatively low vegetable kingdom. Every tree that puts forth flower and foliage with returning Spring exemplifies the law. Ripened fields of grain proclaim its completion; the lichen, "creeping up out of the rock," rejoicing in its new vesture, bears witness to the ebb and flow of the Eternal Motion, the "Great Breath," the Force-Aspect of the Causeless Cause, as it bears on its bosom the myriad hosts of nature elementals, now clothed in objective form, now resting in unconscious subjective arcs of their cycles of existence.

Passing to the animal kingdom, we find the evidences of specific reincarnation becoming more and more pronounced. Other elements of consciousness have been gradually added to the colorless base; differentiation has advanced farther, and anything but specific individual reincarnation has become more difficult in consequence. A distinct step, and one not observed in the vegetable kingdom, is seen in the metamorphosis of insects. Metamorphosis is, of course, but another exemplification of the repetition by nature of steps already taken in attaining a desired end; yet it is more. It shows a deliberate use of the old material, a reconstruction of a new form from outworn matter without permitting a dispersion of this, which plainly proves an unwillingness to enter subjective realms with the material connection entirely severed. As this connection was maintained in the vegetable kingdom by roots, seeds, and bulbs, so here it is accomplished by means of larvæ, pupæ, and perfect insects. Between each stage is a condition of almost perfect subjectivity—a Devachanic interlude from the insect standpoint—followed by the return of the objective arc, which results in reincarnating the same individual in an entirely different body, constructed out of the old material. Form, function, habit, are all so changed that nothing but the evidence of actual observation would convince us that the beautiful butterfly was the actual reincarnation and re-embodiment of the repulsive caterpillar.

It is interesting to note the preparation for metamorphosis, and its significance in several directions. Newport, quoted in Duncan's "Transformation of Insects," thus describes the process:

"When a full-grown larva is preparing to change into the pupa state, it becomes exceedingly restless, ceases to eat, and diminishes much in weight. Many species spin for themselves a covering of silk, termed a cocoon, or case, in which they await their transformation. Others prepare little cavities in the earth, and line them with silk, for the same purpose; and some suspend themselves by their hindermost legs to the under surface of a leaf. In each of these instances the important change takes place in the same manner. Before the larva thus prepares itself for metamorphosis, its alimentary canal is completely evacuated of its contents; its body becomes dry and shriveled, and much contracted in length; and certain enlargements at the sides of the anterior segments indicate the now rapidly developing parts of the future pupa.

"The larva of the butterfly either fastens itself by a little rope of silk carried across its thorax to the under surface of some object, as a ceiling, etc., or suspends itself vertically by its hind legs, with its head directed downwards, as is the case with the common nettle butterfly *Vanessa urticæ*. We have watched the changes with much care in this insect, which frequently remains thus suspended for more than ten or twenty hours before the transformation takes place. When that period has arrived, the skin bursts along the back part of the first segment, or mesothorax, and is extended along the second and fourth, while the coverings of the head separate into three pieces. The insect then exerts itself to the utmost to extend the fissure along the segments of the abdomen, and, in the meantime pressing its body through the opening, gradually withdraws its antennæ and legs, while the skin, by successive contortions of the abdomen, is slipped backwards, and forced towards the extremity of the body, just as a person would slip off his glove or stocking. The efforts of the insect to entirely get rid of it are very great; it twists itself in every direction, in order to burst the skin, and when it has exerted itself in this manner for some time, twirls itself swiftly, first in one direction and then in the opposite, until at last the skin is broken through and falls to the ground, or is forced to some distance. The new pupa then hangs for a few seconds at rest."

After the formation of the pupa case, in describing pupa life, the author continues:

"In all insects which undergo complete metamorphosis this is the period of quiescence and entire abstinence. Many species remain in this state during the greater part of their existence, in others it is the shortest period of their lives."

That is to say that all the wonderful changes which transform a crawling, slimy caterpillar into a glorious vision of beauty and freedom take place in silence and darkness, "from within without," in the absence of all that

food supply which is so necessary to the "scientific" conception of the generation and continuation of "vital" force.
With how little waste of matter nature accomplishes this
conformation of external form to internal idea, is shown
by the fact that a pupa weighing some 71 grains immediately after its transformation in August, in the following
April weighed over 67 grains, "having thus lost but 3.7
grains in the long period of nearly eight months of complete abstinence."

In the higher planes of the animal kingdom, metamorphosis of the entire organization practically ceases; the
remnants of it which persist being limited to organs rather
than bodies, as in the transformation of the water-breathing
tadpole into the air-breathing frog, through the metamorphosis of the respiratory apparatus, together with that of
locomotion.   The long abstinence from food among
insects in the pupa state is also found in a modified form
in some of the higher vertebratæ, as in the various hiber-
nating animals, and in the fasts of reptiles, in all of which
the consciousness practically retires to subjective realms.

Yet in this kingdom the most important advance made
is in the substitution of the egg for the seed as a *point
d'appui* for the reincarnating entity.*   The clinging to the

---

*That is, the highest *point d'appui*.   The fact that the lowly forms
of both animal and vegetable life approach each other so closely that
even the microscope oftentimes distinguishes with difficulty the
kingdom to which a given specimen belongs, only shows that entities
from either kingdom use the same protoplasm with almost identical
results in form-building in these lowly beginnings.   It is, also, a magnificent illustration and confirmation of the fact that there is an inner
spiritual essence, and not an outer material force, causing the primal
appearance and subsequent evolution of form; for under the latter
hypotheses there is no possible explanation why two cells apparently
molecularly identical should diverge, the one into the vegetable, the
other into the animal kingdom.

material form in the latter has been boldly abandoned, and a minute speck of protoplasm substituted. This shows that the entity has evolved to a point of greater differentiation— has acquired greater confidence, as it were. It also affords room for greater variation; as the soul, whether animal or human, is not rigidly bound by a form already partly constructed in advance. Greater freedom is thus afforded it in modifying its own tenement; and the evolution not only of more perfect forms, but of a greater diversity of organs in the same form is provided for. The balance of evolution has distinctly swung to the spiritual or Conscious-Aspect of nature; the middle point has been reached in the animal and passed in the human kingdom.

To sum up, it is plainly evident that consciousness ensouled in the mineral kingdom has the mineral stamp impressed upon it, and is limited by this until it struggles out as a zoöphyte or lichen, under the pressure of the general evolutionary impulse. In this kingdom, reincarnation as a universal process can only occur at the birth of a new world, and every such birth is a reincarnation of a previously existing planet which has died. There is no creation in its ordinary sense possible in nature. Matter, Force, and Consciousness are equally indestructible, and uncreate.

In the vegetable kingdom, specific reincarnation of plants takes place under the ebb and flow of the natural, cyclic laws known as the "seasons." In the animal, the metamorphosis of insects absolutely proves the re-embodiment of the same conscious entity in an entirely different organism, under an inner, subjective force, unaided by external conditions. And between the creeping caterpillar and the beautiful butterfly there is certainly a vaster difference in form and function than is necessitated on any plane by the conscious entity, or soul, merely passing from body to body through the medium of intervening subjective states.

Efflux and influx, subjectivity and objectivity, follow each other in unending succession, and are universal in nature. Life succeeds death, to again give place to its opposite when the subjective arc of the cycle is reached. The periods occupied by their alternations are infinitely varied, as well as the degree to which the one state is replaced by the other. It is easy to trace the beginning of these subjective and objective alternations in the vegetable kingdom into and through the animal, and to observe them becoming all the time more pronounced and, apparently, more disconnected from each other. But we have seen that this disconnection was only apparent, and not real; that the same entity was merely passing through the subjective arc of its life-spiral during the period we variously term root-life, metamorphosis, hibernation, sleep, and death. It has been shown that the monadic base, the Ray from the Conscious-Aspect of the Causeless Cause, being of necessity uncolored and attributeless, has attributes and limitations impressed upon it by the various material experiences it passes through, and the widening of its conscious area, as a result of this. We have noticed that as this consciousness is widened each addition, to the human state at least, increases limitation and intensifies individualization, so that the range of possible choice in reincarnation becomes all the time more restricted. Thus an entity that could choose from the whole mineral kingdom, in the vegetable might be limited to a genus, in the animal to a species, and in the human to a family.

Now, if the individualization of a tulip, even, has proceeded so far that nature has expressly provided for subjective cycles of the same individual, by the evolution of a bulb, how much more reasonable it is that the intense individualization in man should also be conserved by subjective periods in his life history. That the conditions limiting his consciousness in each state are different is no argument against these existing. The consciousness of a butterfly differs vastly from that of a caterpillar; nor does the butterfly ever know of the caterpillar state, as far, at least, as we can judge. The two are quite separated in time. It logically follows, then, that the individualization, carried to so marked an extent as it is in man, should be provided with subjective periods in which to assimilate and make its own the experiences of the last physical life. It is also reasonable that this experience, being so widely varied, should be best assimilated under conditions of entire subjectivity. If, as Plato declares, "the soul reasons best when least harassed by the bodily senses," so much the better will it garner the wisdom taught by the fleeting panorama of its past life when entirely free from physical perturbation.

Then, if everything in nature is pointing towards and preparing for distinct periods of subjective experience in the cycle of human existence, we can hardly be wrong when assuming that reincarnation is fully and completely proven by this preparation for and gradual leading up to it on her part, for again the truism meets us that *natura non saltet*, and it would be a great deal more than a leap for her to suspend processes once inaugurated. It would be like a great river, whose waters have been collected from the four quarters of a continent, suddenly ceasing to flow and disappearing into nothingness when within sound of its aim and end, the sea.

CHAPTER VII.

THE COMPOSITE NATURE OF THE SOUL.

THUS far, in our study, we have spoken of that which reincarnates in man under the generic term of Soul. It now becomes necessary to use a more specific expression, in order that we may determine just what portion of man reincarnates, and what does not. This can only be accomplished by a study of that composite nature of man's soul which is evidenced by the complex character of his conscious functioning.

All systems of philosophy, with the sole exception of that which passes for a philosophy under the name of modern Materialism, recognize the complex nature of man, and all classify this complexity as a necessary step in any philosophic analysis of his being. In the Kabala, Gnosticism and Buddhism, the division is into seven Principles or basic elements entering into his composition; in Vedantin Brahmanism and the teachings of Lao-Tse, there are five; in Christianity, three— the body, soul and spirit, of Paul; while Materialism alone recognizes but one, the "matter" of his body, and of which all his other faculties are, according to it, but properties.

Without pausing to examine wherein other systems agree or disagree with the theosophic classification, we will take up that as being identical with the exoteric enumeration of several great religions, and as agreeing esoterically with all of them. This is the seven-fold division, and corresponds with other great septenates in nature. It separates man into Body (Sthula Sharira); Astral Body (Linga Sharira); Vitality (Prana) ; Animal Soul (Kama); Human Soul (Manas); Spiritual Soul (Buddhi); and Spirit (Atman). The words in paren- theses are the Sanscrit originals, of which the English equivalents are attempted translations.

From this classification it is at once apparent that " soul " may be defined as any vehicle for conscious- ness, as was shown in the opening sentences of this work; and the necessity for an accurate technology is seen to be imperative. For in the above enumeration there are three Principles classed as " souls," each being a vehicle for a higher expression of consciousness, while the Body and Astral Body fall, strictly speaking, under the same category, both being also but vehicles for other states of consciousness.

Let us begin this necessarily brief examination with the lowest principle, or the Body. Under the evolu- tionary and philosophic necessity, as previously pointed out, of higher, more developed centers of consciousness, using matter already the seat of consciousness in lower expressions of form, it is at once seen that the Body represents in its molecular constitution hosts of these lower lives. Every cell is a synthesized group of such lives; every organ, a synthesized group of cells; every system, a synthesized group of organs; every Body, a synthesized group of systems. Now, a synthesis demands—and demonstrates—a synthesizer. So it is evident that man, even in his lowest, most material aspect, or Body, represents hosts of such synthesizing centers of consciousness. That each cell is an entity, even science freely admits. Green, for example, in his " Pathology and Morbid Anatomy," states:

" Ever since Schwann discovered the cellular nature of animals, and established the analogy between animal and vegetable cells, there has been a gradually increasing conviction among physiologists, which has now become a universally accepted physiological and pathological doctrine, that the cell is the seat of nutrition and function ; and, further, that each individual cell is itself an independent organism, endowed with those properties and capable of exhibiting those active changes which are characteristic of life. Every organized part of the body is either cellular, or is derived from cells, and under no circumstances do they originate *de novo*."

This is directly confirmatory of Weismann's theory of an immortal cell handed down from parent to offspring, from modifications of which, by the countless elemental lives actively engaged in the construction, maintenance and repair of his body, all that magnificent structure is formed. It has an important bearing, as will be shown when dealing with the Reincarnating Ego, upon the karmic relation of the Thinker to his body; this immortal cell being the actual physical basis for the transmission of physical heredity.

The Body, then, is simply a molecular and cellular association of lower " lives," of various degrees of consciousness, synthesized and used by the Thinker, the true Reincarnating Ego, as a necessary bundle of sense organs to relate its higher consciousness to this lower plane.

The Linga Sharira, or Astral Body, is the ethereal counterpart of the gross body; the location of the centers of sensation; and the vehicle of Prana, the Life Principle, upon one side, and of Kama or desire, upon the other. The philosophic and logical necessity for such a body is abundantly demonstrable, yet space limits to the consideration of phenomenal proof alone. These consist in dreams, in " döpplegangers," in

"materializations," in "repercussions" of injuries in-
flicted during "materializations," in the "physical manifestations" of mediums in (low) clairvoyance, in "ghosts,"
"wraiths," and apparitions, etc.   The complete hypothetical proof of the existence, by necessity, of such
a body is to be found in certain phenomena of hypnotism.
It is well known that hypnotizers can prevent their subjects from seeing any person or object which the hypnotizer designates by simply willing or "suggesting" that
upon awakening they can not.   This prohibition may be
made to extend to any or all of the senses, at pleasure.
Thus, is one instance, the "subject" was made unable to
see the body of a person present, but was permitted to
see his hat.   This resulted in an apparent movement of
a hat through space without any perceptible cause,
greatly to her astonishment and dismay.

Now, it is at once apparent that if the centers of
sensation are located in the physical cells of either
retina, optic nerve, or thalami, nothing but an actual
physical interposition of matter upon their own plane
can possibly inhibit their action.   Given that physical
cells convey the result of a vibratory impact along
physical nerve tracts to physical ganglia, and we have
a physical sequence that only physical means can possibly
disturb.   This, too, without noting the further factor in
the problem of purely mechanical motion having been
transmuted into terms of sensation—an impossible phenomenon with a purely physical circuit.   Nothing but
degenerative disease, or the surgeon's knife, can interpose
any barrier between the vibration and its translation into
terms of sensation, if the whole sequence have actually
been limited to the physical plane.   Therefore, when

phenomena force us to admit the fact of such inhibition
we are also forced to postulate this "inner man" as the
only possible explanation. Its presence, also, is, as we
have seen, proven by hosts of other phenomena, and it
is thus not compelled to rest its claims for recognition
solely upon a hypothetical necessity. But given a Linga
Sharira, having within it centers of sensation for the
reception and transmutation of molecular vibrations,
which centers respond and yield to the will, then a
stronger will can interpose between the soul and such
centers of sensation, with the results brought out by
hypnotism, the phenomena of which is thus satisfactorily explained. This will be more fully seen in the
chapter devoted to the bearing of hynotism and Mesmerism upon the phenomena of consciousness.

The Linga Sharira is formed of "matter" immediately
above or "within" that of the physical earth. It disintegrates with the body, of which it is, as stated, an
ethereal counterpart, whose office is to furnish a connecting link between man's inner Ego and the coarser
physical molecules.

The third human Principle is Prana; vaguely recognized
by science as "vitality," because of the constant occur-
rence within the human organism of phenomena exceeding the possibility of being explained by any "natural"—
i. e., materialistic—law. It is the phenomenal aspect of the
universal Life Principle in the Universe; or of that which
Eastern philosophers call *Jiva*. *Jiva* is but one of many
terms for the Force-Aspect of the Causeless Cause; the
latter being objectivized as the "Light" the "Life," or the
creative power of the Logoi. There is no point in space
where this *Jiva*, or "Light," is not potentially present;

when it becomes a potency, it is transmuted into Prana. Thus Prana is not the life principle in man alone, but also that of every entity in the material universe, whether that entity be ensouled in the mineral kingdom as a stone, in the vegetable as a plant, or in the animal or human kingdoms as individual members of these natural divisions. Jiva and Prana are one; Jiva becomes Prana when apparently refracted and differentiated by matter or Substance.

The fourth human principle is Kama, or desire. Like all the others, this is also an universal principle in nature. It finds its point of grossest and most material expression upon the fourth plane of the Cosmos, and upon the seventh sub-plane, or the human-animal plane. In its highest aspect, Kama is that pure, untainted spiritual Compassion-Desire which brings the objective universe into activity, that it may again permit subconscious entities to take up their evolution towards freedom from limitation. In its lowest aspect, it is reflected in the "loves of the atoms" by which molecular association becomes possible. In animals and animal-man, it is a raging, irrationalized, insatiable selfishness; the cause of that apparently cruel "struggle for existence," which we observe in the kingdoms below us; and which, alas! is also but too evident in that of man.

All entities in the Cosmos, at some stage in their becoming, reach and pass through this intensely kamic plane—a plane only in the sense that, being a real "property" of matter, entities having reached it exhibit in the matter with which they clothe themselves this quality of Rajas, or passion. As we can not believe in any deliberate cruelty in nature, the kamic stage must therefore be a

necessary and beneficent one. It may be the means of
so concentrating and individualizing centers of consciousness and nascent souls as to permit of their being lifted
as individualities to higher planes. It certainly affords an
efficient school of instruction in the Pairs of Opposites of
Eastern Philosophers, and thus permits and enforces the
widening of man's conscious area. As it will be further
dealt with in connection with the Reincarnating Ego, it is
passed by for the present.

The four principles enumerated, and which are commonly classed as the Lower Quaternary, are thus seen to
belong equally to man and to the kingdoms below him. In
them alone there is nothing to distinguish man from the
animals, nor does this Quaternary reincarnate in the specific sense in which we speak of the reincarnation of the
human soul. Upon the death of a man, as the microcosm
of the Macrocosm, he of necessity goes into a pralaya, or
subjective existence, corresponding accurately to that of
the Cosmos. For when the Great Cycle is completed,
when the hour of universal dissolution strikes, the "body"
of the Cosmos, or matter upon this molecular plane, first
disintegrates. The consciousness ensouled by it becomes
subjective, or "latent"; a bare potentiality of again manifesting, when similar conditions again present an opportunity. Next, plane after plane of entities ensouled with
higher conscious centers is reached by the touch of
Brahma-Siva, and each in turn becomes also a bare potentiality during the eons of Non-Being which constitutes the
Great Pralaya. At last those are reached which have
evolved to the point of eternal self-consciousness. The
latter, therefore, pass consciously into these eternally subjective planes. An analogy might be thought of thus:

Suppose a cold wave were to gradually pass from the poles to the equator, freezing every plant, animal, and man into a stony rigidity, but not destroying their potentiality of again manifesting all their former activities should the cold wave pass away and permit the old climatic conditions to be restored. Let us suppose this frigid condition to last for ages, after which it does pass away and again permits of the resumption of active life by the inhabitants of each successive zone as the wave of cold recedes northward. If we further conceive of this process of successive suspension and regaining of consciousness as eternally repeated, and that entities overtaken below the plane of subjective self-consciousness have no conception of the interval passed in the frozen condition, we may dimly imagine that which takes place upon all the ' planes below self-consciousness at the out-breathing and in-breathing of the "Great Breath," or the great Cycles of Being and Non-Being. Only that in this pralaya it is consciousness which must be thought of as frozen or latent, if below the plane of subjective self-consciousness; and not form, as in the illustration given, for all form disappears under the power of the In-Breathing of Brahm.

Similarly, upon the death of the body, the cell-forms disintegrate, and the entities ensouled by them become "frozen," or latent. Their Great Pralaya has struck; their Prana re-becomes Jiva; their "matter," now the abode of lower, unsynthesized lives alone, enters the general storehouse of nature, or, rather, returns to the plane from which it had been temporarily lifted by this association, and may be and is used over and over again for similar purposes by other entities. The Linga Sharira, which is but finer ethereal matter, surrenders its Prana, and is similarly resolved back into its component lower "lives." The higher kamic "elementals," those which synthesize the various "organs" of the body, are next reached by the "inbreath," and become latent—changing into those *skandhas* of Vedantin philosophy which await the return of the soul to incarnation, which is their manvantara, or opportunity for renewed conscious manifestation.

Thus the whole of the four lower principles take no part in reincarnation as self-conscious entities. There yet remains that which is termed the Higher Triad to deal with, which completes the Septenary classification.

Of these the most important (to us) is the Reincarnating Ego, the Center of Self-Consciousness; that which Mrs. Annie Besant first termed the Thinker, which is the real basis of man's apparent and (relatively) true individualized existence. But as this will be dealt with in a separate chapter it will be passed for the present, and the remaining two briefly considered.

Sophists have tried to show that the Causeless Cause of Theosophic Philosophy was an impossibility, because the moment any cause is postulated one antecedent and causal to it, as well as one subsequent, are at once required. The Universe, from this point of view, is but an eternal sequence of causes and effects impossible of interruption or cessation. This is a true view of all finite causes and effects. These are a series in which the cessation of one cause as an effect changes necessarily the relation of this to a future one, so that it becomes in turn a cause. Yet if this is true of finite causes and effects, it none the less demands the postulating, philosophically, of

a causal basis which supports the whole finite series without itself being in any way modified or limited by so
doing.   Thus, if the series of finite causes and effects
which we recognize as the manifested or phenomenal
Universe be likened to an immense series of arches
spanning an ocean, the existence and integrity of each of
which truly depends upon its immediate neighbor upon
either side, then the Causeless Cause would be the solid
rock upon which the piers supporting all the arches rest.
That rock is equally undisturbed and unmodified whether
piers or arches rest upon it or not.   And this non-limit-
ation and non-modification is the same, although a portion
of this rock be used in the construction of both piers and
arches.   In like manner, the Causeless Cause remains
unmodified, although it is both the base upon which phenomenal existence rests and that phenomenal existence
itself (as one aspect of its manifestation).

The Atman, the highest human principle, is a Ray from
the Causeless Cause, and thus defies definition and eludes
analysis.   It is the base upon which man's Thinking principle rests its phenomenal existence.   It is the pier which
supports the arch of a human soul.   But it also equally
supports and is the base of all things in the Universe as
well.   It is the Unknowable Something, or No-thing,
rather, which binds together those properties which constitute alike Matter, Force, or Consciousness.   Thus in
gold we have certain properties, as ductility, malleability,
weight, cohesion, extension, etc.   Now, what has caused
these various properties, this malleability, ductility, cohesion, etc., to unite into atomic form as gold?   Is it
chance, or is there an unifying, synthesizing, causal base,
upon which all the properties of any so-called matter

can equally rest? Theosophy declares for the latter proposition, and further insists that the varied and multiform qualities and faculties of man's divinely complex mind are also synthesized by and rest upon a Ray from this same Causeless Cause. This Unknowable Ray, then, is Atman, and bestows potentially upon man by virtue of its origin all the Creative, Preservative, and Destructive (or regenerative) powers we see manifested in the Universe about us.

But a Cause without an agent to bring about its effect is inconceivable—at least, to all but Western materialistic philosophy. Therefore, as we see in nature an obvious duality in spirit and matter, and recognize that any absolute law must obtain on all planes of the Cosmos, we must also postulate a material aspect or vehicle for this Atmic Ray. It is as undefinable and metaphysical as Atman itself, but it is an absolutely necessary philosophic hypothesis. It also arises as a perfectly legitimate logical sequence in following physical laws into metaphysical domains. This vehicle, for Atman, then, is called Buddhi, and, like Atman, is an universal, indestructible principle potentially present in every conceivable point of space, and, like the latter, its apparent separation in man or nature· an illusion.

Yet we would err were we to look upon this base of the material aspect of man's being as being only material. There is no pure matter in the Cosmos, as there is also no pure spirit. And as each expression of consciousness, under the law of cause and effect, must seek a fitting vehicle, Buddhi, being the vehicle of the Atmic Ray from Absolute Consciousness, is of itself possessed of faculties and powers infinitely superior to man, even in his highest aspect of a Thinking, Reincarnating entity. As the vehicle of Absolute Wisdom and Power, it is called the Knower, in superior contradistinction to that Thinker next it which has to arrive at knowledge and wisdom by thought or reason. As the vehicle of Absolute Consciousness, it corresponds, in its relation to this, to the human brain, or man's physical basis for registering conscious experiences. In the latter are recorded all his conscious experiences in matter during a physical life. In Buddhi is stored, as corresponding to an eternal, metaphysical brain of the Universe, the conscious experiences of all manvantaras. To reach the wisdom residing in this Divine Vehicle, to widen one's conscious area to Infinite bounds, is to become immortal in very truth, for it is union with that which is One and Indestructible. Such an union is undoubtedly attainable, but before its attainment stretch such immeasurable vistas of time, such inconceivable experiences in consciousness, that at our present stage speculation upon it seems unwarranted. The union of the lower Personality with the Higher Ego is our present evolutionary task, the relation of which to each other and to nature will be next considered.

CHAPTER VIII.

THE REINCARNATING EGO.

WE have now reached a point where we may perhaps profitably study the nature and function of man's Fifth Principle, omitted in the general review because its importance required a more extended and careful consideration. This Principle is variously spoken of as Higher Manas, the Reincarnating Ego, the Thinker, and other names. It is the true individuality, as contradistinguished from the lower, fleeting personalities of its successive incarnations. It represents that aspect or power of the Absolute which causes individualized centers of consciousness to first form and then to attain to self-consciousness in the Phenomenal Universe. It is this Principle which reincarnates, for it alone represents the true man. The Quaternary disappears as an entity at death. Buddhi and Atman are universal non-individualized Principles; Manas, the Thinker, alone journeys as a self-conscious entity from body to body by means of Reincarnation. This Thinker, then, in its various relations to the body, and especially in its aspect as the Lower Manas, or the personal self, remains, after all possible elimination of other factors, as of prime and paramount importance in the problem of human existence. Let us study it carefully and reverentially, for in and through it alone shall we be able to come into an understanding of the Divine in nature and in man; for they are One.

There has been shown, in the chapter devoted to the

evolution of, the soul, the gradual process by which an atomic center of consciousness, through continuous conscious experiences, attains to the self-conscious, or human stage, while on its way to godhood. We have also seen that the law of cyclic periodicity shows how and why such centers are graded into great hierarchies, by the natural limits thus set to their emergence from the bosom of the Absolute. The relation which the Reincarnating Ego bears to this world and its cycle is thus capable of logical solution.

It is evident both phenomenally and philosophically that the material Universe is embodied Consciousness, or Consciousness of infinite gradations, clothed in equally infinite expressions of form. As the Universe ebbs and flows—to finite perception—from subjective to objective states throughout the eternities of Duration, it follows that worlds appear and disappear endlessly; the Great Prayala, even, being only a subjective arc of larger immensity. In the life history of all worlds, as is proven by the records now visible in the heavens, there comes a time when they cool down sufficiently to become habitable; when they pass through this stage; when, by the ebbing of their life force, or the completion of their limiting cycle, humanities can no longer exist upon them in material form. There is no doubt but that their minor pralayas, or deaths, overtake them with the consciousness of their entities in states of infinite diversity, such as we now perceive upon this earth. Hence, there would be Egos passing through the human stage overtaken when their world became uninhabitable for them; for the life cycle of a planet pursues its course perfectly uninterrupted and uncontrolled by the evolution of any humanity upon it, although the two always correspond. Similarly, were pralaya to strike for this earth to-day, would all entities, human, animal, or elemental, be arrested in their material evolution and be compelled to remain in subjective states until other worlds arrived at stages capable of affording them expression in suitable material forms.

Our Higher Egos have witnessed, it is claimed, the death or pralaya of many such worlds, for matter on our own physical or molecular plane, by its power of illusion, and by the ease and rapidity with which its unstable nature permits of disintegration and the entering of the out-worn constituents into new combinations, is evidently a very important, if humble, school in a Universe where every entity " is, was, or prepares to become a man."* Planetary pralayas, therefore, have overtaken our Higher Egos, it may be a great number of times; for who can estimate the period necessary in material states of consciousness for them to arrive at their present stage ?   At any rate, when their last world went into pralaya they had not yet passed beyond the desire for material or sensuous existence, and so were, under the law of cause and effect, drawn to human-animal bodies which nature, through its lower hierarchies of " Builders," had been preparing for their occupation during those interminable periods which geology is beginning to recognize as necessary factors in human evolution. This reincarnation of already highly advanced Egos of former worlds in human-animal forms, prepared for them under the physical aspect of the triple-sided process (physical, intellectual, and spiritual) of evolutionary activity upon this world, is the key of the whole scheme of human

*Secret Doctrine.

evolution upon this planet.　It also solves many otherwise hopelessly insoluble problems in human consciousness, such as clairvoyance, prophetic dreams, and the "buried selves," so strangely dug out of their unsuspected graves by hypnotic processes.　All such phenomena, as we have seen, prove that there is in man's body a soul too superior to that body to be the product of the same evolutionary process which has produced its transient tenement of clay.

Man's Higher Ego, then, as shown by its possessing powers and faculties far transcending its material vehicle, must be the product of former world periods.　Because of its derivation from the Conscious-Aspect of the Absolute, as a Ray from Mahat or the Cosmic Mind, the Reincarnating Ego is a center of potential self-consciousness upon all the planes of nature in the Cosmos.　This potentiality has, during these former manvantaras, become a potency upon many of these planes, some of which, as shown by the Divine Wisdom of the Higher Ego, must be infinitely superior to the sensuous consciousness of this earth.　It now seeks cosmic perfection by the evolution or attainment of this same, or perfect, self-consciousness, upon all planes of the Cosmos yet remaining unexplored.　For Self-Consciousness is the aim, the end, and the crown of consciousness upon any plane, whether material or spiritual.

Being a Ray from the Absolute, emanating as it must from that Causeless Cause lying hidden behind all manifestation, the Higher Ego possesses the creative and ideative functions involved in its own emanation, or creation.　This creative power in the Reincarnating Ego— creative in the sense of changing or renewing form only

—is most important to bear in mind. It must not be supposed that ordinary men consciously create—a power reached by Adeptship alone; or even that the Re-incarnating Ego consciously creates or builds its own bodies: that again is only possible for those in whom the Higher and Lower Egos have become one. But the Reincarnating Ego does build astral and thought forms unconsciously, under the potency of that power or force which is carried with it in its emanation from the Cause-less Cause. This creative power is the source of the Linga Sharira, the second human principle; within which the physical molecules which constitute the Sthula Sharira, or physical form, are moulded. It is also the source of all thought forms, from the "Mayava Rupa," the consciously constructed "illusion body" of the Adept, to those airy forms and scenes which in dreams change and shift even while we gaze upon them, so unstable and feeble is the action of the will in these unrecognized, faint functionings of a soul thus unconsciously exercising creative faculties.

In harmony with all nature, the Reincarnation of the Higher Ego occurs in regular cycles of alternating ob-jective and subjective existence. Its objective arc is earth life; its subjective is termed Devachan.* With the return of the Higher Ego to incarnation, when its sub-jective cycle of existence in Devachan is ended, the Linga Sharira for the new physical body which is to be built becomes an active, formative potency. It awakens into activity all those elemental or "skandhic" forces, in enforced pralaya during the devachanic interlude. Con-ception having taken place, these and still lower hier-

---

*Devachan.   See chapter on Post-mortem States.

archies of Builders begin to mould physical cells within the astral model, so furnished. Here and now occurs the first struggle with matter and material limitations which attends all the subsequent conscious experience of the Ego in the new body. Under the awakening presence of the Higher Ego, the hierarchies of Builders, called by scientists—though very unscientifically—"natural forces," must set to work; but this work is very greatly modified because of the stamp upon the physical cells by the parents of the physical form, under the law of physical heredity, the lowest phase of the triple evolution before referred to. On the other hand, this physical impress is again modified in a greater or lesser degree by the urgent tendencies of the Higher Ego to express certain dominant qualities under the force of "skandhas" of past incarnations. Unmodified by a Higher Ego, man would represent the exact average of the sum of his parents' qualities, both physical and pyschic, as is seen in the almost endless continuation of identical forms in the vegetable kingdom and in the lower animal—in mollusks, for example. Unmodified by physical heredity, the Higher Ego would have no real karmic hold upon earth. As experience is an absolute necessity for development, the struggle with this physical impress given by parents under the law of physical heredity affords the opportunity required to develop the Higher Ego's functions and potencies upon this plane of consciousness. It also satisfies the law of cause and effect, or Karma, which compels Egos with certain characteristics to seek parents having similar ones, for growth must always proceed from the present point of attainment. Did physical heredity not modify the habitation and powers of the Reincar-

nating Ego, there would be no reason' why it should
seek expression through one parent rather than another,
and we would be forced back upon the unjust Christian
hypothesis of the human soul having no voice in the
selection of its body. Did not the Reincarnating Ego
have the power to very greatly modify its material
tenement, the faculties and psychic powers of the child
would represent the average of the sum of those of its
parents at best; and the innumerable instances where
these are very greatly transcended, as well as those
where the account is on the debit side, would be wholly
unaccounted for.

It is thus apparent that man's soul and body are each
the exact complement of the other. The relation of the
one to the other becomes explicable, and is but another
illustration of the absolute play of cause and effect, or
of action and reaction, between the material and spiritual poles of the One Reality. Intellectual, or Higher
Ego, heredity brings over the results of man's entire
conscious past; physical heredity enables him to begin
further evolution or widening of consciousness at the
exact point where he left off, and along just those lines
where his spiritual need is greatest. Thus a man in
a body full of any of the lower, *rajasic* qualities pro-
claims to the world that his Higher Ego has need to
further evolve their opposites, and such instances ought
to arouse all our sympathies—call forth our best brotherly
efforts, rather than that contempt and aversion which we
are too apt to experience. It is as though we were to
turn shudderingly away from a pure, saintly prisoner
because the cell in which he is confined is loathsome.

Physical heredity is thus explained: There are, according to Weismann, certain cells in man's body which have never died since his appearance in a physical form upon this earth. These cells are, necessarily, according to him, transmitted directly from parent to offspring, and actually carry forward those physical qualities which constitute purely physical heredity. But it is not necessary to predicate an eternal cell, although this is possible and probable. It is enough that actual, physical matter is so transmitted, for no possible division of matter into smaller particles can destroy or even diminish its physical properties. The great and all-important quality of matter is to register and record conscious experiences obtained by material associations. Upon tablets of some degree of materiality all conscious records must be graven, even though this be the *Mulaprakriti* of Eastern, or Primordial Substance of Western, Philosophy.

At conception, there is an actual fusion of cells from the father with others from the mother, thus forming one cell, the type of all life. This cell divides, and subdivides, almost infinitely, for out of its subdivisions, through repeated modifications, all the various tissues of the body are constructed. There is not nor can not be an introduction of a single new or foreign cell in the entire organism. All increase or growth is by division of the original cell, and molecular accretions thereto by means of nutriment supplied—a fact which explains the wonderful selective power the various tissues exercise upon the common food supply. Portions of this original cell are therefore present in every other cell of the body, and by virtue of their registering qualities, carry into the new body the impress of all purely physical experiences or form limitations of both parents. The fusion

of two necessarily differing parental cells gives also the
opportunity and basis for all requisite variation.   As the
matter of the father or the mother predominates, so will
the new body more closely resemble the one or the other
parent.   And back of this, even, a peculiarly strong
physical impression made by an ancestor may dominate
that of both parents, and atavism result, or the same
effect may be brought about by "skandhas" unable to
incarnate previously, and so lying latent.

Thus is seen how powerful is the influence from the
physical line. of heredity, when each cell of the entire
body is tainted with every physical desire, appetite, or
passion of the purely animal nature of both parents.   And
the Linga Sharira, enmeshed in these cells, and being the
seat of the centers of sensation, bring its parent, the
Reincarnating Ego, into direct karmic relations with all
these animal propensities.   It also affords a vehicle for
the re-awakened skandhic elementals to pour their stream
of muddy desires into the physical body; owing to karmic
attraction having drawn the Reincarnating Ego to parents
having similar characteristics.   Thus the physical conformation, the tendency to disease, to a long or a short life,
to repeat such abnormalities as six fingers or toes, or such
peculiarities as red hair or squint eyes, together with
hosts of other purely physical limitations, are the result
of physical heredity, and transmitted by the handing
down from parent to offspring of actual physical matter so
impressed, and with a subconscious tendency to repeat the
original impression.   The emotional and passional nature,
while afforded easy and fitting expression by physical
cells from parents having like characters, appears to be
of skandhic heredity, and carried over in this manner from

former lives. It is a form of physical heredity, it is true, but not purely so, for it abandons one body to reincarnate in another; thus resembling the "seed" reincarnation in nature, while the physical cell heredity is a case of pure propagation by fission. But no mental characteristics can be carried over to the new life thus. As we have seen, the conservation of mental force requires a mental vehicle, so that all purely mental qualities are the result of mental or intellectual heredity, and come by and through the Reincarnating Ego. Mental powers may be and are but too often sadly inhibited, or almost destroyed, by overwhelmingly bad psychic and physical heredity, which retard or prevent their manifestation; but they none the less come through the channel of the Reincarnating Ego alone.

The creative power of the Higher Manas, then, acting upon subconscious planes; produces or creates a Linga Sharira; similarly as on the subconscious planes of the Lower Manas, our personal self, all the vital activities as well as the repair of wounded or diseased tissue, go on quite independently of our conscious supervision.

On its own planes its creative potencies are exercised consciously in the production of those higher astral forms which the Adept uses when he abandons the physical, in his journeyings. With this higher creative faculty mankind at large is not, at present at least, concerned. But since the Higher Manas builds, or rather, causes to be built, its physical body, through creative power thus unconsciously exercised, in what manner is it consciously, and so karmically, connected with the body?

This calls for an examination of its creative functions on ideative or mental planes, or the reflection in matter of

its true, individualizing consciousness. This reflection—
perhaps refraction would be the better term—of itself is
quite another process to that concerned in the formation
of the Linga Sharira, which we have been considering,
and is the most important of all. The Linga Sharira may
be said to represent its purely physical expression, so to
speak; this refraction, the Lower Manas, is itself, mirrored
in material thought processes. The former expresses its
purely physical karma,* or its physical creative force
taking the lines of least resistance; the latter connects it
karmically with the thoughts and mental processes of past
lives. Being, when its devachanic or subjective existence
between two lives is closing, drawn to the parents pre-
senting the greatest sum of karmic affinities, the contact
of the soul with the growing form sets up in the physical brain of the latter a thinking principle similarly as a
magnet upon being brought in contact with non-magnetic
iron imparts magnetism to this, without having caused the
smallest change in those physical qualities which constitute it iron. And, as the evolution of the physical
form, which it took ages for the Elemental Builders, or
the ordinary evolutionary forces in nature, to accomplish,
is repeated swiftly during the first few weeks of gestation,
so is the entire evolution of the Lower Manas also repeated during the first few years of the child's life. For
these Builders only push matter up to the animal or
kamic† plane; the brooding presence of the Higher Manas

---

*Karma—the sequence of causes and their effects. Karmically—
brought about under the law of cause and effect, etc. Used in this
work to avoid cumbersome English phraseology only.

†Kama—Sanscrit for desire, especially associated with animal or
non-intellectualized desire.

must impart the stimulus which brings it where it is of sufficient transparency, so to speak, to receive and refract its image.   It will be at once plain that our Lower Manas, the ordinary self, is thus a portion of the very essence of the Higher, just as the magnetism in the iron is a portion of that in the magnet.   And just as the magnet may be withdrawn from its contact with the iron, leaving a portion of its magnetic qualities to slowly dissipate, so may the Higher Manas be separated entirely from its lower reflection, thus constituting for the latter a veritable "loss of the soul."

For this portion of the Higher Manas actually refracted or incarnated in matter is ourselves, the "I am myself," of our earthly life.   Could it remain simply a portion of the Higher, its functions and fate might be different, but this is impossible.   As the pure ray of light is colored by the color of the glass which transmits it until it is indistinguishable from that tint, so is the Lower Manas colored and changed by its contact with Kama (sensuous desire), the chief and ruler of the earthly Quaternary.   All the fierce desires, the unrest, the sensuous appetites, the "lusts of the flesh," of the latter at once seize upon it, and impart to it that curious mixture of the animal with the Divine which we name the lower self, or Personality.   This could not occur had not the kamic Principle in the lower Quaternary already been evolved to a point where it is not only able to receive the magnetic impress of Manas, but to color this with its own qualities of passion and desire.

It is the opinion of the writer that it must not be inferred from the above that only a portion, as it were, of the Higher Manas incarnates in the lower Quaternary, leaving the rest to enjoy a kind of superior consciousness

upon other planes.   While the teaching is reserved upon
this point, still there is enough given out, in the Secret
Doctrine and elsewhere, to make it reasonably certain that
each individuality has but one center of consciousnesss,
and that this is not in full activity in two places, nor in
two or more states, at the same time.   While it is active
upon one plane it may have a subconsciousness on others,
just as we may be reading and yet be conscious of noise
about us.   But this is only a subconsciousness, not a
splitting of it.   Therefore, when once the Higher Manas
has perfected its vehicle sufficiently to permit this, it
would seem that it only functions through that vehicle
when this is active, for its very activity compels its use as
a vehicle.   In other words, our "I am myself," or individualizing center of consciousness which comes from the
Higher Manas and is its distinguishing characteristic, is
functioning actively only through the body when this is in
the waking state, although its subconsciousness may extend over many higher planes.   When the body ceases
its activity, as in sleep or death, then it can of course retire to its own proper spheres, to be dragged down from
these by its kamic connection with the body when this
awakens.   It follows, then, that when awake and occupied
by material or sensuous thoughts only, the Higher Manas
is simply paralyzed—its consciousness upon this plane a
potentiality only, somewhat, perhaps, like that of the
lower consciousness when inhibited by hypnotism.   This
is its daily crucifixion, and the true meaning of all the religious myths of crucified Saviours.

   Yet, though the Higher Manas be paralyzed as to conscious functioning, it cannot be said to be wholly or even
partially incarnated in the body, nor is it even ever

fully conscious upon this plane except when its Higher and Lower aspects have been enabled to unite, through the latter having conquered in its contest with Kama. The oneness and yet the separateness of the Higher and Lower Manas is one of the hardest of mystic teachings to understand. It is another illustration of the "Same and the Other" of which Plato taught that the Universe was constructed. Perhaps the phenomena of an ordinary Faradic electrical battery may help us, by analogy, to a better conception. In this, the current, generated by the zinc and carbon, or other elements, in the presence of an acid or saline solution, is passed through a coil of insulated wire. Around this, in what is technically termed the helix, is coiled another wire, also completely insulated, and entirely disconnected from the first, or "primary," coil. There ought, therefore, to be no current in this latter, or "secondary," coil, yet the instant the current from the chemical cell is passed through the primary coil there is set up in the secondary at each opening and closing of the primary circuit a modified current, known as "induced" electricity. Because there has been no actual contact between the two coils, this secondary current is thus said to have been produced by "induction"—one of those convenient terms by means of which science seems to explain so much, while really explaining nothing. Without attempting to account for the real origin of this induced current, except to point out that the electro-dynamic waves in the ether, discovered by Prof. Hertz of Bonn, will give all necessary clews, the analogy to the origin of the Lower Manas and its relation to the Higher is very close. The presence of the Higher Manas, overshadowing the body, originates a distinct Thinking Principle in the brain of the

latter, in a manner strikingly similar to the induced current of electricity—that is, by imparting to the latter its
own essential qualities. Thus it can be at once seen that,
while the Lower Manas is caused by and is of the very
essence of the Higher, it is yet distinct without being separate. Withdraw the primary current, and the induced
will disappear; withdraw the Higher Manas, and the
Lower perishes, the chief distinction being in the slower
process in the latter case.

Perhaps a closer analogy to the behavior of the Higher
and Lower Thinking Principles after death is afforded in
the phenomena of transferred magnetism just referred to.
For, in the illustration given, when artificial magnetism
has been imparted to non-magnetic iron, upon the with-
drawal of the true magnet is seen almost identically that
phenomenon which takes place upon the separation of the
Higher and Lower Manas. A portion of magnetism remains in the iron, to be slowly or quickly dissipated, as
the case may be; it having apparently become entangled,
so to speak, in the molecules of the latter, or having, more
correctly, caused a polarized arrangement among those
molecules whose vibratory ratio exhibits the qualities of
magnetism. So, at death, only that portion of the Lower
Manas is withdrawn which is untainted by kama. That
portion colored by kama is left; a residue, having, by
virtue of its original Manasic origin, enough still of the
unconscious creative power, before referred to, to clothe
itself with an astral form; thus constituting the "Kama
Rupa," which, senseless and fallen as it is, is still the
"guide" of many a poor, obsessed "medium." For while
having no center of consciousness capable of feeling and
functioning as such, still it is capable again, by virtue of

its Manasic origin, of having a false feeling of personality reflected into it by the Lower Manas of a medium. This reflection may so synthesize its fading consciousness as to enable it to connect itself with its past life, and to relate the leading events of this quite accurately. Its feeling of "I am myself" is thus an illusion of an illusion, if we may be allowed the expression, for the feeling of "I am myself," which we experience in our waking state, real as it seems, is entirely illusive, being reflected there in a similar manner by the overshadowing of the Higher Manas. It only exists because of its connection with the latter, and is added to the sum total of the experiences of its parent at death, as the memory of each day may be said to be added to the sum of the consciousness of our personal selves. For, having drawn what of wisdom it may from each association with a body, the Higher Manas withdraws at death, taking all of Lower Manas which has freed itself from Kama, leaving the remains of Lower Manas and Kama to disintegrate in Kama Loca.* And as there are many days that leave little or no impress upon the consciousness of our personal selves, so there may be many lives having but small record on the tablets of the Higher Manas, while some may be forgotten altogether.

These forgotten lives are the most dreadful fate which may befall a personality, for they are truly "lost souls." The whole of the reflected portion of the Higher Manas has been sunk so low in Kamic desires and passions that there is no union possible after death; and the Personality, strong by virtue of this robbing of the qualities of its parent, clothes itself in a powerful Kama Rupa and becomes

*See Chapter on Post-mortem States.

an active agent for evil, while at the same time descending its own arc to utter annihilation amidst indescribable suffering, of which the realization of its impending fate is not the least.

We may now, perhaps, dimly perceive the relation between Higher Manas, the Thinker, which, with Atma and Buddhi as a Monadic base constitute the Reincarnating Ego, and Lower Manas, its reflection in matter which constitutes the personal self. The one is the result of the evolution through unthinkable æons of time, of an individualized, spiritual self-conscious soul; a self-conscious Ray from the Great Cosmic Thinking Principle; the potency of Thought in the Atmic Ray individualized. It persists throughout all minor manvantaras and pralayas; through all obscurations or destructions of worlds or systems. Yet of itself it is not immortal. It must become one in essence with Buddhi, the Eternal Knower and Recorder, to win eternal persistence as an individual entity. Similarly, the Lower Manas can only survive one life by becoming one in essence with its source; by freeing itself from the attractions of Kama and returning to its source with the tribute of its conscious experiences in matter to add to the already stored wisdom of the latter. The Lower Manas is thus but the illusory reflection of the Higher, when this has been karmically drawn to a human-animal body by its desire and necessity for complete knowledge of the material and sensuous states of consciousness upon this plane of existence. This reflection, or refraction, thus produced, wins its immortality according as it approximates towards its Divine parent or yields to the sensuous delights of Kama. And not only this, but of even more importance, since personal immortality is more the concern of many incarnations, it determines in each life by its thoughts and acts the social environment, the race, the nation, the family, the intellectual trend and capacity, and the ease or difficulty, even, with which the Higher Manas can control the following life or personality; so intimate is the karmic relation between the two. For while the Higher Manas, as compared to its reflection, is god-like in its wisdom and powers, it by no means follows that it has perfected wisdom on this plane. If it had, the necessity for repeated incarnations might be questioned. And the tendencies of our finite minds is, all the time, to take the finite view of everything—to want to complete and round out the whole scheme and plan of the Cosmos in a few years. This is the pitiful mistake which Christian theology falls into in predicating the completion of man's earthly destiny in one short life. Our Higher Egos may have spent manvantaras in other humanities developing on quite distinct lines from those which we vaingloriously imagine include all possible mental and spiritual characteristics; they may spend manvantaras to come, evolving consciousness along equally unsuspected lines.

Yet, god-like and wise as is the Higher Manas, it has, as we have thus shown, to descend life after life to overshadow, impart its own essence to, and acquire wisdom through and from the human bodies with which it is karmically associated. During the waking states of these bodies it can only function through them by means of its reflection, the Lower Manas, which is thus, for this period, its only conscious avenue for reaching this plane. Yet so dimmed and discolored is the Lower Manas by the desires and passions of kama, that the consciousness transmitted through it by the Higher Ego may well be compared to the light from a sunbeam struggling to penetrate an opaque, densely-stained prison window. To the prisoner within, who has never known any other light, the purity and brilliancy of the source of the dim, scarcely discernible ray, penetrating the gloom of the cell, might well remain a matter of doubt, or even of absolute disbelief. Yet in a precisely similar manner does our Higher Ego overshadow our gross material body, struggling to penetrate and enlighten its inner darkness; whispering to our Lower Soul in the divine voice we recognize as conscience; prompting us to altruistic work for humanity; filling our hearts with its divine compassion; the true source of every aspiration to become purer, wiser, and more unselfish than we feel ourselves to be.

And the task of every human soul is to help in this great evolution of spiritual consciousness; to turn the strength of a purified will consciously to the aid of nature in the warfare between good and evil; between light and darkness; between Life and Death. This struggling, sinning, suffering Personality can only return to and become one with its divine progenitor by freeing itself from all coloring of kama—by the utter killing out of desire. How important, then, a correct conception and realization of the nature, interrelations, and mutual dependence of our Higher and Lower Egos become! By this knowledge, and only by it, is it possible to formulate a theory of ethics, a rule for human action, for right living and thinking, which shall explain why a man ought to strive to be pure, passionless, altruistic; to live in the spiritual portion of his nature; to yield a willing, loving obedience to the dictates of his Higher Self; to treasure each glimmering Ray from its Divine Light, even though it take the form of stern rebuke, as of a million times more value than all the gold of Ophir!

CHAPTER IX.

THE PERSONALITY.

ALTHOUGH considered at some length in the preceding chapter, the lower self, or the man of earthly sorrows, woes, ambitions, appetites and desires, which all of us are while encased in these material vestments, may still, perhaps, be examined profitably as a separate study. The Personality is, as we have seen, the lower Quaternary, or the Man-animal, intellectualized by the incarnation of the Higher Ego, from one point of view, and the Higher Ego itself, benumbed, paralyzed, and its consciousness suppressed or distorted and discolored by the imperfect sense organs of its body, from another. To disentangle and define just what the relation of the Personality to the Higher, Reincarnating Ego is, constitutes one of the most difficult of tasks, and one, perhaps, impossible until man's reasoning faculties are quickened and corrected by intuition. The theory which follows is submitted for consideration, only. It has no authority except that it seems a reasonable hypothesis, in view of the many phenomena it explains.

We have seen that reincarnation is an universal law; that it obtains on every plane and in every kingdom of nature. It has also been shown that it is always specific, and occurs under the law that not only do causes produce their inevitable effects, but that like causes produce like effects. In other words, the cause must not only be equal to the effect, but must correspond to this effect in essence or nature. Material causes can not originate conscious effects, and *vice versa*. For this reason, all re-incarnation must be specific; each class conserving its own differentiation of consciousness. An animal must reincarnate in the animal kingdom, and in some species like to itself in character. Thus the conscious center of a tiger, for example, must reincarnate in an animal having similar characteristics.

The condition of these animal centers of conscious-ness between incarnations bears also upon the problem. It has been stated that they become latent; but this is a vague term. It must not be understood that they lose their identity as conscious centers. The term "latency" is used to distinguish their state from the devachanic one of the human soul. In the latter, consciousness does not cease to function, but only transfers the scene of its ac-tivities to inner or subjective planes. In animal souls, the consciousness becomes a potentiality only; it ceases to exist as an active potency even on subjective planes. That consciousness is capable of this cessation of activity, or change of the mode of its manifestation, is abundantly shown by analogous phenomena on the physical plane. Thus, oxygen and hydrogen, when combined as water, cease to exist as gases, without at all losing the poten-tiality of again returning to gaseous states when their as-sociation as water is terminated. This mysterious ability to retain a primal potentiality throughout infinite sequences of later correlations and associations is another key to the mystery of evolution, and the manner in which everything in the Universe may philosophically and ac-tually have its source in Absolute Unity. For if hy-drogen and oxygen can combine to form water, so, also, can water be decomposed into hydrogen and oxygen

again. It is, therefore, evident that not only can everything in the Universe arise out of Unity, but that the reverse is also true—that all things can be resolved back into
Unity with equal certainty.

This latent condition of animal centers, then, is a retiring of such centers into states where, though their
identity disappears as a potency, it is preserved as a potentiality. It is the state to which all mineral, all vegetable, and most animal conscious centers retire. It is as
near an approach to the primal monadic consciousness as
the evolution of these centers will permit. But, as all
planes of consciousness pass gradually into those above
and below, so, also, in the higher animals are there evidences of the beginnings of subjective states. Dogs,
canaries, etc., undoubtedly dream, and this ability must
include the power to maintain a subjective existence for
brief periods after death. In other words, many, if not
most, animals have a stage in their life cycle corresponding, in a lower degree, to that of Kama Loca in man.

It will now have become apparent to what all this leads.
Since animals have a subconscious center, or "elemental,"
which persists as an entity not only through latent states,
but also through real subjective ones as well, it is plain
that the human animal also has such an "elemental," only
of higher degree. This "human elemental" is, evidently,
the source to which we have to look for the next
humanity, in a becoming which is necessarily infinite in
duration. It is this nascent human center which flames
up under the intellectualization of its animal desires into
the larger portion of that which we recognize as the "personality." When the rationalizing presence of the lower
Manas is withdrawn by death, it is this entity which runs

riot during the brief period of its ability to maintain a subjective existence in Kama Loca, both before and after the Higher Ego passes into the tranquillity of Devachan. It is its still raging desires which at first disturb and prevent the devachanic rest of the soul. It, also, is able to flame up again under the influence of the Lower Manas of a "medium," when, of course, it may often give correctly facts concerning its past life, and especially those so powerfully impressed upon it by the manner of the death of its body.

Yet there is in it no "I am I," except it be reflected there. It has not evolved to this point by many cycles. That which each one feels as his "I am myself," if his consciousness be upon the material plane and concerned with sensuous desires, is only a reflection from the Higher Ego, faintly shining through the intellect of the human-animal. It is thus an illusion, and must remain so unless one can so hush the clamors of the senses as to permit his consciousness to rise to its own divine plane. Withdraw Manas, and the "brain-mind" collapses, all sense of "I am myself" disappears, and the human "elemental," after gathering itself together as the "spook" or "Kama-Rupa," for a brief period of uncanny subjective existence, becomes "latent"; retiring from even subjective thought planes until a new reincarnation enables it to become a potency by clothing itself once more in a human-animal form.

Within this human-animal reside all sensuous passions, desires, and appetites; all those "qualities" of rage, greed, cunning, and hosts of others, which the Hindoo philosophers class as "*rajas*" and "*tamas.*" Western theology would fain have us believe these lower "devilish" qualities to be inherent in man's true or spiritual nature. They are a part of its conception of "original sin," and, truly, a "vicarious atonement" by an omnipotent god is necessary if these are really constituents of our spiritual being. But the Eastern metaphysicians fall into no such error. These qualities are foreign to and impossible of existence upon the spiritual planes of the Higher Ego; so much so that they can not even be impressed upon its divine memory. They can only be experienced by proxy, as it were, or by the Higher Ego incarnating in an animal form where these have their normal plane of activity.

From its own plane, the Higher Ego brings its own native powers. Intuition or direct perception of truth, justice and virtue; complete unselfishness; prophetic power; and so on, may be taken as types. It is also the source and plane of true self-consciousness. By its simple presence it intellectualizes the lower *rajasic* appetites and passions, thus rendering them a thousand-fold more difficult to subdue. The process is, as we have seen, similar to the contact of the magnet imparting magnetism to non-magnetic iron. But to intellectualize only is not its mission. It must spiritualize these lower qualities, and transmute the experience so acquired in the contest into a knowledge of their "opposites," which can be recorded and preserved on its own divine plane.

All the "qualities," all the passions, desires, appetites, and intellectual powers, even, of purely animal man are to be found in varying degrees in the lower animals. As an animal, man in no way differs from other animals except in degree, and this degree, in many of the lower instincts, is relatively and actually lesser in him. If one were to attempt a diagrammatic illustration of the effect

upon animal man of the incarnation of his Higher Ego, it
might be shown first in what the "quality" consisted
upon the animal plane, what it becomes when merely intellectualized, and what when spiritualized or transmuted.
Thus, in its highest animal type the

		INTELLECTUALIZED.		SPIRITUALIZED.
Cunning of the	Fox,	Becomes Cheating;		Inventive Skill,
Vanity	" Peacock,	"	Love of Dress;	True Self-Respect.
Ambition	" Eagle,	"	Desire of Fame;	Desire for the Advancement of the race.
Greed,	" Swine,	"	Love of Riches;	Altruistic Desire.
Rivalry,	" Horse,	"	Wars, Prize F'ts;	To help others succeed.
Cruelty,	" Tiger,	"	Slave-Driving. Wage-Robbing;	Indifference to Personal Suffering.
Mechanic Skill of the Bee,		"	Palace Building,	Philosophy Building, Higher Mathematics, etc.

The Personality, then, in its lower aspect, is this human-
animal rationalized by lower Manas. Yet the presence
and action of the latter must not be overlooked in our
too close study of the lower aspect, or we shall have, at
best, but an one-sided conception of our lower self.
Through the various Principles which connect the
Thinker, the Higher Ego, with the body, and especially by means of lower Manas, the Higher Ego is able
to project rays of its own divine ideation upon the
brain cells; to infuse its consciousness into the "brain-
mind," and so purify by its own golden light the muddy
flames of brain intellectuality. The voice of conscience
is a message direct from this divine inner sufferer and
prisoner, who knows by virtue of its own native powers
the ethical bearings of any doubtful question or transac-
tion. There is no need for time to consider or reason;
the judgment is instantaneous and unmistakable; the soul
is before the tribunal of its own divinity; for the brief moment the warning voice is heard.

If, then, there be no "I am myself" in the Personality

except as reflected there by the presence of the Higher
Ego, thus " clothed in a coat of skin," thus "crucified in
the bonds of flesh," it is at once evident why there can be
for it no immortality. The lower aspect which has
flamed up under the vivifying presence of the Higher
Ego, as the dimly burning flame of a night lamp might
under the impetus of a jet of pure oxygen, fades into bare
latency after death. It can not endure even as a
memory; for its passionate cycle of existence is not nor
can it be recorded in the memory of the Divine Inner
Ego. The Higher Ego retires to subjective planes, and
in Devachan assimilates the wisdom acquired in its last life
on earth. All is gone—the lower aspect of the Personality to the oblivion of latency, the higher to its source.

How, then, is any immortality possible for the Personality? Only in the memory of the Higher Ego of the
period during which it spent a life cycle in such or such a
body is any record preserved. The association is remembered as the memory of such or such a dwelling occupied
by man during one life might be. Illumined by some
noble act, some self-sacrificing deed, how the memory of
all surroundings shines forth out of the obscurity of
common-place, selfish existence! Every detail remains
vivid; the act and all its accessories of environment or
circumstance are accurately preserved.

So with our Personalities. It is possible to so illumine
our life with noble and unselfish deeds and thoughts that
it shall remain a vivid and pleasant memory to our
Higher Ego throughout eternal vistas. It is, also, possible to permit the consciousness of our divine Self to be
so drowned in the clamor of the senses, to be so suppressed by a wicked, selfish, or even a vain or idle life, that

no record is preserved. Such a life is a day in which "nothing happened to us"; forgotten, not because of this, but rather because we permitted it to pass without making it live in our memory by some good deed done to our fellow-men.

Such will be the fate of most of the Personalities now upon the human stage. The biblical warning, "Behold, they are neither hot nor cold, therefore will I spew them out of my mouth," contains an occult truth it would be well to ponder. The memory of such lives will be taken to Devachan, to be dreamed over and their foolish fancies enacted in pleasant, illusory "castles in the air," and the soul will then be returned to earth for renewed opportunities to live a higher, nobler life. But beyond Devachan such lives can not pass. There their cycle terminates forever as surely as that of the animal soul terminates in latency. It can not be too strongly impressed that only truly spiritual or unselfish deeds survive in the eternities of the memory of the Higher Ego, for like causes can only produce like results. Animal, earthly, or kamic causes can not be followed by spiritual effects; the stream can not rise higher than its source.

There is yet one aspect of the Personality which must be considered before we can fully, or even partially, grasp its entire functions and potencies. This is the possibility of its complete separation from the Higher Ego through deliberately choosing the low, sensuous plane of the Quaternary, and the cruel, conscienceless struggle for existence which there has its normal field of activity. By stifling the voice of the Higher Ego, or conscience; by allying itself to evil; by vice and crime committed with the full realization that they are vices and crimes—there becomes possible for the Personality the fate of its utter and entire extinction. The *rationale* of this may be readily understood by what has already been explained as to its post-mortem history. We have seen how intensely the presence of the Thinking Principle, the Reincarnating Ego, rationalizes those which before were merely animal passions and desires. If, now, the Higher Manas fail entirely to spiritualize these, the "I am myself" of such a person is only that of an animal—more cunning, more selfish, more conscienceless and more cruel, by a thousand fold, than if the Higher Ego had never incarnated within it. The whole of the energy aroused and imparted by the latter is absorbed by the human animal. Instead of burning for a time in Kama Loca, like the smoking wick of a candle whose flame has been extinguished, this being enters this plane at death with all its potencies for evil in full activity. No Devachan is possible; and as all its desires rage furiously earthwards, their very force will carry it speedily to a new reincarnation, and we then have a Jesse Pomeroy, or a Deeming, horrifying mankind by his atrocious crimes. So great may have been the impetus, so powerful the energy thus robbed from Manas, that a series of these human-animal incarnations may occur, each more soddenly brutal than the last, until an incarnation such as a jabbering idiot at the end prefaces the final plunge into animal latency. As a nascent center of human consciousness, the human-animal Personality can not be destroyed; but it is evident that it can so cut itself off from the Higher Ego upon one hand, and from the natural evolutionary activities of the upcoming animal monads upon the other, that it is quite separated from all chance of progress during incalculable periods. For the same widening of the area of its evil nature which cut it off as unlike and unassimilable by the Higher Ego, also made it unlike and superior in evil to the kingdom below; and it can not, therefore, re-enter this. Of its fate, however, after it has lost all of its borrowed glory, and after it no longer recognizes itself as the man who had once the opportunity to become divine, it is useless to speculate. It is enough to know that the sufferings of such a Personality must be awful, indescribable. For whether he reincarnate immediately, or whether, this reincarnation being for karmic reasons impossible, he obsesses poor "mediums," to their ultimate sharing of his fate, alike must he expiate to the full every crime or evil thing done during the time he forged the chains which bound him to so terrible a destiny.

This is a fate which can overtake every human Personality, and the fact should be known as an evolutionary possibility. There are too many evident failures upon the purely physical plane—too many infant deaths—not to make it plain by correspondence and analogy that there may be also failures upon the menfal plane. Let each one who considers himself too far over the line of danger pause, and seriously question himself as to whether his life is lighted by the pure flame of spirituality, or whether he is not, after all, living an unsuspected life of merely animal emotions, instincts and appetites, intellectualized to such a brilliancy that the glow may prove a false beacon light to the ultimate wreckage of his soul ; for it can not be too often nor too strongly insisted upon that no amount of mere intellectuality removes us from the animal plane to the safety of spiritual existence. Altruism is the law; compassion, the means; self-sacrifice, the surety, of existence upon the stable spiritual planes of being.

The monadic base upon which our center of consciousness rests is alone eternal and immortal. Our Higher
Ego depends for its immortality upon rising to this
monadic base in its conscious functioning. In a much
greater degree is the personal Ego dependent upon the
Higher for its promise of eternal life. All turns, as we
have seen, ·upon the plane in which the personal " I"
habitually functions; upon how deeply it permits itself to
be dragged below the Divine plane to that of mortal passions and desires. Meanwhile, as our Higher Ego gathers
strength and expands its consciousness through this experience of many lives, its reflections in material incarnations, or personal " I am I's," become also stronger, and
the loss of any one of them through having been overcome by sensuous attraction grows more serious, both to
Higher Ego and lower personality. For the mutual reaction and interdependence of the (Higher) Ego free and
the (lower) Ego incarnated, are very great, or successive
incarnations under the iron law of cause and effect would
not take place as they now inevitably do.

CHAPTER X.

POST-MORTEM STATES OF CONSCIOUSNESS.

SINCE a recognition of the truth of the continuous evolution of the soul by means of Reincarnation precludes all such puerile and childish conceptions of Post-mortem states as the Christian's "heaven" and "hell," the Spiritualist's "Summerland," or the materialist's blank negations, it becomes necessary to examine into this phase of the Ego's existence from the view-point of the larger philosophy. As few men have evolved the ability to consciously penetrate during life to those inner planes where the Reincarnating Ego of necessity retires upon the death of its physical body, itfollows that the teachings concerning the Post-mortem states of consciousness are somewhat *ex cathedra*. Nor is there anything derogatory to intellectual dignity in accepting statements of this nature from those who are in a position to know as sufficient evidence of the facts. We willingly accept the statements of astronomers, mathematicians, chemists, etc., as to facts beyond our reach physically, and often above our perception intellectually, because they are known to be experts by virtue of study along these particular lines. We are under equal obligations to accept information or facts concerning the spiritual aspects of our being from known students and experts in these fields. Both classes of data are equally capable of personal verification—the one by the exercise of our intellectual, the other by our spiritual, faculties. And spiritual truths at first veiled by spiritual blindness may be perceived later by persistent cultivation of the spiritual faculties, for growth and power follow exercise of these as certainly as that using the hammer enlarges and strengthens the biceps of a blacksmith.

However, information and knowledge concerning these post-mortem states are not, purely, nor even largely, *ex cathedra*. The teaching has all the authority of a philosophic hypothesis which fully explains and synthesizes the phenomena within its proper territory. Were there no other reason for accepting it, the fact that it explains the chaotic phenomena of "spiritualism" would alone entitle it to our respectful consideration; and when to these are added large classes of cognate and quite unclassified supersensuous facts, it may be said to rest upon a strictly philosophic and scientific basis.

The Theosophic classification of these Post-mortem or ante-natal states is into Kama Loca, Devachan, and Nirvana—terms borrowed from the Sanscrit because of the want of accurate English synonyms. These are simply, states of consciousness, dependent upon the relation of Ego to its material vestments and environments. Our ordinary waking consciousness is dependent upon and conditioned by the sense organs of the body, being the result, as pointed out in the chapter upon the Physiological Evidence of the Soul, of innumerable molecular shocks or changes arising chiefly without, but also within, the organism. Deprived of sense organs by death, consciousness depends upon the ability of the Ego to function upon interior planes of ethereal substance. The ordinary man has not evolved to the point of being able to do this, so that after complete separation from his lower and more truly "material" principles his consciousness becomes subjective—a state analogous to pure dream, and undisturbed by any real, objective phenomena whatever. Before reaching this state of pure subjectivity, however, the consciousness has to pass through a process of gradually abandoning these lower vehicles. This condition of mixed objectivity and subjectivity is termed Kama Loca; that of pure, dreaming subjectivity, Devachan; while Nirvana may be defined as consciousness upon planes so far interior to this one of molecular matter that he who enters it self-consciously can never return to lower worlds— loses all possibility of response to molecular vibration. All are in their nature and essence subjective states of being, as, indeed, all consciousness necessarily is. The Conscious-Aspect of the Causeless Cause ever appears subjective in its relation to the Substance-Aspect, its material vehicle.

Since physical consciousness is manifested on the physical plane of matter, which latter to our senses is certainly a place, in like manner Kama Loca consciousness, being limited to the lower astral plane of substance, may also be understood as connected with locality, that locality being the Linga Sharira of the earth. But these associations of locality are not essential. The place where consciousness is experienced is nothing; the state itself, everything.

All states of consciousness, too, may be actually experienced while the body is on the physical plane, and all have their physical correspondences in our ordinary waking consciousness. An Arhat attains to Nirvana while yet in the physical body; because he has, through the efforts of his trained will, risen beyond the limitations of this vehicle for purely sensuous consciousness. An ordinary man experiences Devachan on earth. The day-dreamer, building "castles in the air," very closely approximates this condition, because his mind has cast off, for a time, its material fetters, and functions on an inner and more spiritual plane. The sensual and passionate man finds himself very closely approximating the Kama Loca state when yielding to the angry impulses of his lower nature, for the reason that his consciousness is then limited to the physical correspondence of that plane. The analogous states of day-dreaming, anger, or passion, are not accurately identical with Devachan or Kama Loca, for the reason that with the former states there is always the modification of the Thinking Principle through its connection with the body, while in the latter this union is severed by death, and the impeding action of our physical senses due to physical stimuli is withdrawn. Still, we will be best able to understand the nature of the real Kama Loca and Devachan by a close study of their physical analogies, for, as we have said, they are the actual states, excepting for this modification by the physical body and lower principles. It is the one center of consciousness, modified by the vehicle which expresses its dominating condition; while in the body, if in a passion, the Animal Soul, or vehicle for the expression of this form of mental energy, is of necessity used—as a mechanic is compelled to take up a different tool when he wishes to cut from that he uses for polishing only. On the other hand, this passional vehicle could not be employed for devachanic day-dreams; one can not build castles in the air while in a furious passion.

It must not be understood from the above that the Higher Ego ever gets into a passion, or in any similar emotional state, itself. All these passional activities belong to the consciousness of the various hierarchies synthe-

sized in man's body. The kama-manasic reflection of the
Higher Ego is the agent by means of which the latter is
brought into sense relations with this plane, and this center of consciousness vibrates from one to another of these
vehicles under the impelling influence of the personal will.
This personal will is the reflected will of the Higher Ego
tainted and colored by the desires and delights of sensuous existence. It is thus the offspring of the personal
or kama-manasic consciousness, and represents the underlying motive which directs our whole personal existence.
It is created by kama-manasic or brain thought, which
thought arises out of the physical stimuli of sensuous existence. Thus is seen the nature of the intimacy between
body and soul, and also the importance of controlling the
kama-manasic or lower brain thought, or of not permitting
these sensuous stimuli to engross the entire attention of
this center of consciousness. "As a man thinks, so he is."
If we continuously find ourselves getting into rages, it is
not, as most of us delude ourselves into fancying, the result
of an unhappy combination of environing circumstances,
but because we live habitually upon this level. If our
desires really ran in the direction of purity and spirituality,
the same set of circumstances would arouse no corresponding vibrations within us; we would be non-receptive
to them, as completely as we now are to the ultra-violet
rays of the spectrum. Through all the psychic storms
raging in the body, the Higher Ego is only a spectator,
powerless to affect the result except as its lower reflection
controls or yields to the tempest of vibrations arising in
these rajasic elementals.

The effect of permitting the center of consciousness to
wander from plane to plane, according as this or that desire

demands a hearing or clamors for its attention, is more far-reaching than is generally recognized. It is the karmic agent which is largely determining the conditions of our next subjective life as well as the following incarnation.

Perhaps a resort to object teaching may help to elucidate this. Let us suppose man to be living within a hollow sphere or globe, modeled after the fashion of that he now lives upon. Let us further suppose this globe to have a north and south pole—that is, a spiritual and material extreme. An equator would then divide its upper spiritual from its lower material hemisphere. Below this equator would be the physical and Kama Loca consciousness; above, the devachanic and nirvanic. At the upper pole would be the ethereal, spiritual attraction of his Higher Self; at the lower, the kamic desires of his physical body, and each constantly exerting its utmost power to draw his kama-manasic center of consciousness to its own pole. This kama-manasic center of consciousness may be likened to a smaller globe, ever oscillating within the greater one. Now it floats, under the impulse of some altruistic, spiritual impulse, far above the dividing equator into the spiritual region. In an instant it descends to material zones, as some earthly desire or fit of passion reaches it through the physical senses. Thus it ever vibrates to the impulses arising out of sensuous experiences unless controlled by the will, crossing the dividing line between the spiritual, permanent life, and the fleeting, physical one, perhaps a thousand times a day. With some exceptionally spiritual natures, the oscillation may be within the devachanic zone of consciousness for days or weeks, without ever touching the fatal equatorial line of animal appetites or selfish interests. On the other hand, a gross sensualist or materialist might keep his consciousness oscillating entirely below the line of spirituality for months, or even a lifetime.

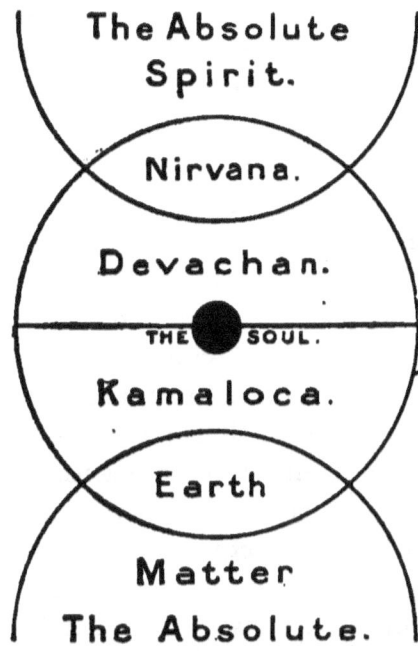

The Absolute
Spirit.

Nirvana.

Devachan.

THE SOUL.

Kamaloca.

Earth

Matter
The Absolute.

Carrying our illustration a step further, let us suppose this larger, or environing, globe to have the power of responding to and recording each visit made by the smaller globe, representing the kama-manasic consciousness, to any of its planes or zones, either devachanic or those of Kama Loca or Nirvana. Let us suppose, also, that this record takes the form of a kind of mental or thought-deposit within the greater globe, and which, under the accretion of numberless visits, grows into a thought fund, so to speak —a memory-deposit, upon which the Higher Ego can draw in order to maintain a conscious connection with, or memory of, its last life on earth, during the interval which must elapse in Devachan before it can again descend into the world of causes by reincarnating.

This fanciful thought-deposit roughly represents a fact in nature; for just as our physical brain responds to and records molecular vibrations, so do spiritual thoughts and desires set up vibrations upon higher planes, and which are recorded upon their permanent tablets. These illustrations, crude and imperfect as they of necessity are, enable us to catch a glimpse—a shadowy conception, at any rate—of the mutual inter-relation and interdependence of our life upon earth and that which awaits us after death. By them may be seen how we are daily and hourly creating the conditions which, without the arbitrary interference of any personal god, will determine our state in the next or subjective phase of our existence, as well as the conditions which will environ our next objective life.

After death, when the physical vehicle of consciousness is destroyed, the soul, if it have not evolved the power of objective consciousness upon the inner, astral planes, is compelled to continue its existence in a subjective state. A blind man cannot see, nor a deaf one hear; they lack the physical organs.   Therefore, when all of man's physical senses are annulled by death, either his consciousness is annihilated, as the materialists claim, or it uses inner senses to project the astral plane objectively, or it must become subjective—that is to say, it must enter upon a dreaming state similar to that which obtains during life when the physical senses are paralyzed by sleep.   Then what happens after death, returning to our globe illustration, would evidently be this: The grossly physical attraction at the lower pole being removed, the consciousness rises to that point in the globe where its mental deposits during life have been of sufficient amount to sustain it.   It can no longer select its material vehicle by the self-conscious will, for this has become paralyzed by the disintegration of the lower Principles, through which it had been accustomed to function, and through its not yet having learned to function on spiritual planes and in spiritual vehicles. If, now, the devachanic accretions preponderate, it floats to this zone, and remains until it has received its reward for, or rather exhausted the effects of, the altruistic and elevating thoughts and aspirations of its last life. If the Kama Loca deposits are in excess, there the consciousness remains until, having succeeded in separating itself from these, it rises to its devachanic stores, or, having none there, it again returns to earth and reincarnates, or slowly fades out upon this plane. But this preponderance of deposits does not mean simply an accurate physical or mental balancing of accounts—a casting up of a debtor and creditor column. If this were so, few, perhaps, would reach Devachan. But, just as the material attraction was greatly in excess during life, through the physical or sensuous connection, so now the spiritual forces at the upper pole exercise a correspondingly increased influence when no longer counterbalanced by the body; so much so that Devachan is the almost universal state of the human soul after death. For the personal consciousness, the " I am I," not to be drawn into the safety of Devachan means, as we hinted above, the most terrible fate for it—its utter and entire extinction. Remember, the poles of our globe have more attributes than being merely higher and lower, or outer and inner. The great the all-important difference consists in that the one is eternal and everlasting, and the other mortal and impermanent. Therefore, we see but too plainly how that soul which has cultivated none but grossly material affinities during life will find itself overpoweringly drawn down into the abyss of matter and destruction at death. This is the true and esoteric meaning of the scriptural injunction to "lay up treasures in heaven." For the phrase, " Where a man's treasure is, there will his heart be also," has a real and awful significance when read by the light of Theosophic teachings. Herein is found the explanation and meaning of that mysterious tenet running through all religions—the possibility of the eternal loss of the soul, which will be referred to later.

It might be supposed that, since most souls live to a great degree upon the plane of sensuous desires, thereby laying up treasures of a highly undesirable nature, yet, as they pass almost without exception into the devachanic state after death, the effects or karma of these evil acts were thus avoided. Not so. This is just the mistake that Christianity makes when it translates its repentant murderer from the gallows to eternal bliss, by means of its unphilosophical and unjust vicarious atonement. Theosophy commits no such blunder. As the soul, having experienced the spiritual effects of the spiritual causes set up while in the body, or, having received its devachanic reward, descends to reincarnate in another body, it meets and carries forward to the new account the unbalanced debt of evil, in the shape of the skandhas of its former life. It is these which, following the reincarnating soul into its new body, largely determine the selection of that body, through the law of karma. As Madame Blavatsky explains, in relation to these skandhas, or karmic results of evil acts :*

"They are destroyed as the working stock in hand of the personality; they remain as karmic effects or germs, hanging in the air of the terrestrial plane, ready to come to life as so many avenging fiends, to attach themselves to the new personality of the Ego when it reincarnates."

Thus we see the perfect justice and reasonableness of

*Key to Theosophy.

the Theosophic conception of these post-mortem states, as well as why we are daily and hourly influencing and determining our future states, both in and out of our future bodies. The man who finds himself in a diseased or deformed body, or a member of a depraved family, can not, in the light of karma, charge it to accident, nor injustice, nor to carelessness nor indifference on the part of some god, but must recognize it as a result of these karmic " fiends"—these unexhausted causes created during his past incarnation—which, having been set up there, have followed him into the only plane where they could be satisfied—that of physical life.

After death has separated the soul from its body, what is it that enters Kama Loca, and what that enters Devachan? Man is constituted, as we have seen in its proper connection, of seven Principles, or vehicles for consciousness. To briefly recapitulate, these are : The physical body; its vitality, or Prana; the astral model of the physical body, or Linga Sharira; the passional center, or animal soul, common to man and the animals, called Kama; the human soul, or Manas, having a higher and a lower aspect; the spiritual soul, or Buddhi; and Atma, or pure spirit. The three latter form the upper spiritual Triad, or the true reincarnating Ego. The remaining four form that which is known as the lower, or material, Quaternary. At death the body returns to the matter, or " earth," from whence it came; the vitality, or Prana, rebecomes one with its source—the *Jiva*, or One Life; the Astral Body, or Linga Sharira, slowly fades out, also returning to its source   The soul abandons these three Principles at once and forever when the body dies. But the consciousness still clings to kama—is still, though deprived of

kamic organs, kama-manasic, by reason of its long association with the body. There are thus, immediately after
death, five Principles, including the dual aspects of Manas;
in Kama Loca, where at once a process of separation begins. The clamor of the senses is stilled; and, no new impetus being given to Kama, its vibrations cease gradually
to command the Ego's attention, and the latter becomes
slowly separated or freed from the influence of this
vehicle. Until this separation is accomplished, Devachan
is impossible. When it is, which may take from a few
moments to many years, according as the relative
strength of the material or the spiritual in the soul, the
higher Triad, with all of the late personality worthy of immortality, enters Devachan as a Triad, leaving two more
Principles, or vehicles to become *skandhas* in Kama Loca.
Thus we see man has become from a septenary on earth,
a Triad in Devachan; to rebecome a septenary upon his
next reincarnation. In other words, the true man puts
on a new body, just as he does here a new suit of clothes,
only that the union is more intimate. It is as though one
could not see without glasses, nor hear without a trumpet,
etc., when all of these accessories would become part of
his necessary clothing. In a similar way his lower Principles, or vehicles, simply relate him to matter, clothe him
with a "coat of skin," by means of which he is brought
into sensuous contact with material things.

The Ego, then, must remain in Kama Loca until it is
freed from sensuous desire, and fitted for the quiet bliss
of dreaming Devachan. The actual states of consciousness immediately after death are thus described by
Madame H. P. Blavatsky:*

*Lucifer, Jan., '89

"The Ego receives always according to its deserts. After the dissolution of the body, there commences for it either a period of full,
clear consciousness, a state of chaotic dreams, or an utterly dreamless sleep indistinguishable from annihilation; and these are the
three states of conscionsness. Our physiologists find the cause of
dreams and visions in an unconscious preparation for them in our
waking hours; why cannot the same be admitted for our *Post-
mortem* dreams? I repeat it, *death is sleep*. After death there begins before the spiritual eyes of the soul, a performance according to
a programme learned and very often composed unconsciously by our-
selyes, the practical carrying out of *correct* beliefs or illusions which
have been created by ourselves. A Methodist will be a Methodist,
a Mussulman, a Mussulman, of course just for a time—in a perfect
fool's paradise of each man's creation and making."

This is the key-note to these Post-mortem states as
struck by a Teacher. We find no foolish nor impossible
heaven nor hell described, but states analogous to and
built upon our subjective life while in the body. Death
is truly a sleep, wherein the dreams are pleasant or horrible according as we lay the foundation for them while
in the physical form.

But all Post-mortem, or even all subjective life, must
not be included with those which are analogous to sleep.
The opposite poles of being have a common state for the
Ego—that of being awake or vividly self-conscious; only
at the material pole it is the personality or Kama-Manasic
consciousness which is awake, while at the spiritual pole
it is the Individuality or Reincarnating Ego, which is in
this acutely self-conscious condition. To the consciousness at either extremity, that of the other seems, perhaps,
like sleep as compared with its own. But the intervening
Kama Loca and devachanic conditions are a true sleep, as
compared to both poles; only in Kama Loca the dreams

will be "chaotic," while in Devachan they will be as bright and as beautiful as the imagination of the Ego is able to construct out of the material stored up from the altruistic efforts, the spiritual aspirations, and the highest idealizations of its past life.

Passing, now, to the separate consideration of the consciousness in Devachan, it is evident that, being entirely subjective and self-created, in a manner exactly corresponding to dreaming creations while in the body, no two devachanic experiences can be the same. The distinction of individuality remains as sharply drawn as while in the body. On attaining consciousness in Devachan we will take up our old life in our dream, without the faintest suspicion that its continuity has been interrupted. But how changed! Pain, suffering, hardships and sorrow will all have disappeared, as before a magician's wand. Again, as pointed out by Madame Blavatsky :*

"Devachan is an absolute oblivion of all that gave pain or sorrow in the past incarnation, and even oblivion of the fact that such things as pain or sorrow exist at all. The Devachanee lives its intermediate cycle between two incarnations, surrounded by everything it had aspired to in vain, and in the companionship of every one it loved on earth. It has reached the fulfillment of all its soul yearnings. And thus it lives throughout long centuries an existence of unalloyed happiness which is the reward for its sufferings in earth-life. In short, it bathes in a sea of uninterrupted felicity, spanned only by events of still greater felicity in degree."

"It is with those whom it has lost in the material form, and far, far nearer to them now than when they were alive. And it is not only in the fancy of the Devachanee as some may imagine, but in reality. For pure, divine love is not merely the blossom of a human heart, but has its roots in eternity. Spiritual, holy love, is immortal,

---

*Loc. cit.

and Karma brings sooner or later all those who loved each other with
such a spiritual affection to incarnate once more in the same family
group.   Again we say, that love beyond the grave, illusion though
you might call it, has a magic and divine potency which reacts on
the living.   A mother's Ego filled with love for the imaginary children it sees near itself, living a life of happiness, as real to *it* as when
on earth—that love will always be felt by the children of the flesh.
It will manifest in their dreams, and often in various events—in
providential protections and escapes, for love is a strong shield, and
is not limited by space or time."

The devachanic consciousness is also most lucidly explained by another MASTER* of Eastern Wisdom.   He
writes:

"Devachan is not, cannot be, monotonous; for this would be contrary to all analogies and antagonistic to the laws and effects under
which results are proportionate to antecedent energies.

"There are two fields of casual manifestations: the objective and
the subjective.   The grosser energies find their outcome in the new
personality of each birth in the cycle of evoluting individuality.   The
moral and spiritual activities find their sphere of effects in Devachan.

"The dream of Devachan lasts until Karma is satisfied in that
direction, until the ripple of force reaches the edge of its cyclic basin
and the being moves into the next area of causes.

"That particular one *moment* which will be most intense and upper-
most in the thoughts of the dying brain at the moment of dissolution
will regulate all subsequent moments.   The moment thus selected
becomes the key-note of the whole harmony, around which cluster
in endless variety all the aspirations and desires which in connection
with that moment had ever crossed the dreamer's brain during his
lifetime, without being realized on earth,—the theme modelling itself
on, and taking shape from, that group of desires which was most intense during life.

"In Devachan there is no cognizance of time, of which the Devachanee loses all sense.

*See Notes on Devachan by "X," in THE PATH, Vol. V, pp. 40
and 80, *et seq.*

"(To realize the bliss of Devachan or the woes of Avitchi you have to assimilate them as we do.)

"The *a priori* ideas of space and time do not control his perceptions; for he absolutely creates and annihilates them at the same time. Physical existence has its cumulative intensity from infancy to prime, and its diminishing energy to dotage and death; so the dream-life of Devachan is lived correspondentially. Nature cheats no more the *devachanee* than she does the living physical man. Nature provides for him far more than *real* bliss and happiness *there* than she does *here*, where all the conditions of evil and chance are against him.

"To call the Devachan existence a 'dream' in any other sense than that of a conventional term, is to renounce forever the knowl-. edge of the esoteric doctrine, the sole custodian of truth. As in actual earth life, so there is for the Ego in Devachan the first flutter of psychic life, the attainment of prime, the gradual exhaustion of force passing into semi-consciousness and lethargy, total oblivion, and—not death, but birth, birth into another personality, and the resumption of action which daily begets new congeries of causes that must be worked out in another term of Devachan and still another physical birth as a new personality. What the lives in Devachan and upon earth shall be respectively in each instance is determined by Karma, and this weary round of birth must be ever and ever run through until the being reaches the end of the seventh Round, or attains in the interim the wisdom of an Arhat, than that of a Buddha, and thus gets relieved for a round or two, having learned how to burst through the vicious circle and to pass into Para-nirvana.

"A colorless, flavorless personality has a colorless, feeble devachanic state.

"There is a change of occupation, a continual change in Devachan, just as much and far more than there is in the life of any man or woman who happens to follow in his or her whole life one sole occupation, whatever it may be, with this difference, that to the Devachanee this spiritual occupation is always pleasant and fills his life with rapture. Life in Devachan is the function of the aspirations of earth life; not the indefinite prolongation of that 'single instant,' but its infinite developments, the various incidents and events based upon and outflowing from that one 'single moment' or moments. The dreams of the objective become the realities of the subjective existence. Two sympathetic souls will each work out its own devachanic sensations, making the other a sharer in its subjective bliss, yet each is dissociated from the other as regards actual mutual intercourse; for what companionship could there be between subjective entities which are not even as material as that Ethereal body —the Mayavi Rupa?

"The stay in Devachan is proportionate to the unexhausted psychic impulse originating in earth life. Those whose attractions were preponderatingly material will sooner be drawn back into rebirth by the force of Tanha. [Tanha—desire for sensuous existence. J. A. A.]

"The reward provided by nature for men who are benevolent in a large, systematic way, and who have not focused their affections on an individual or speciality, is that if pure they pass the quicker for that thro' the Kama and Rupa lokas into the higher sphere of Tribuvana, since it is one where the formulation of abstract ideas and the consideration of general principles fill the thought of its occupant.

"Certainly, the new Ego, once that it is reborn (in Devachan), retains for a certain time—proportionate to its earth life,—a complete recollection of his life on earth, but it can never visit the earth from Devachan except in reincarnation.

"'Who goes to Devachan?' The personal Ego, of course; but beatified, purified, holy. Every Ego—the combination of the 6th and 7th Principles—which after the period of unconscious gestation is reborn into the Devachan, is of necessity as innocent and pure as a new born babe. The fact of his being reborn at all shows the preponderance of good over evil in his old personality. And while the Karma [of Evil] steps aside for the time being to follow him in his future earth reincarnation, he brings along with him but the Karma of his good deeds, words, and thoughts into this Devachan. 'Bad' is a relative term for us—as you were told more than once before— and the Law of Retribution is the only law that never errs. Hence all those who have not slipped down into the mire of unredeemable sin and bestiality go to the Devachan. They will have to pay for their sins, voluntary and involuntary, later on. Meanwhile they are rewarded—receive the *effects* of the causes produced by them.

"Of course, it is a *state*, so to say, of *intense selfishness*, during which an *Ego* reaps the reward of his unselfishness on earth. He is completely engrossed in the bliss of all his personal earthly affections, preferences, and thoughts, and gathers in the fruit of his meritorious actions. No pain, no grief, nor even the shadow of a sorrow comes to darken the bright horizon of his unalloyed happiness: for it is a *state of perpetual 'Maya.'* Since the conscious perception of one's *personality* on Earth is but an evanescent dream, that sense will be equally that of a dream in the Devachan—only a hundred-fold intensified; so much so, indeed, that the happy Ego is unable to see through the veil of evils, sorrows, and woes to which those it loved on earth may be subjected. It lives in that sweet dream with its loved—whether gone before or yet remaining on earth; it has them near itself, as happy, as blissful, and as innocent as the disembodied dreamer himself; and yet, apart from rare visions, the denizens of our gross planet feel it not. It is in this—during such a condition of complete Maya—that the souls or astral Egos of pure, loving sensitives, laboring under the same delusion, think their loved ones come down to them on earth, while it is their own spirits that are raised towards those in the Devachan.

"Yes, there are great varieties in the Devachan states, and all find their appropriate place. As many varieties of bliss as on Earth there are of perception and of capability to appreciate such reward. It is an ideal paradise; in each case of the Ego's own making, and by him filled with the scenery, crowded with the incidents, and thronged with the people he would expect to find in such a sphere of compensative bliss. And it is that variety which guides the temporary personal Ego into the current which will lead him to be reborn in a lower or higher condition in the next world of causes. Everything is so harmoniously arranged in nature—especially in the subjective world—that no mistake can be ever committed by the Tathagatos who guide the impulses.

"Devachan is a 'spiritual condition' only as contrasted with our own grossly material condition; and, as already stated, it is such degrees of spirituality that constitute and determine the great varieties of conditions within the limits of Devachan. A mother from a savage tribe is not less happy than a mother from a royal palace, with her lost child in her arms; and altho', as actual Egos, children prematurely dying before the perfection of their septenary entity do not find their way to Devachan, yet all the same, the mother's loving fancy finds her children there without one missing that her heart yearns for. Say it is but a dream; but, after all, what is objective life itself but a panorama of vivid unrealities? The pleasure realized by a red Indian in his 'happy hunting grounds' in that land of dreams is not less intense than the ecstacy felt by a connoisseur who passes æons in the rapt delight of listening to divine symphonies by imaginary angelic choirs and orchestras. As it is no fault of the former if born a 'savage' with an instinct to kill—tho' it caused the death of many an innocent animal—why, if with it all he was a loving father, son, husband—why should he not also enjoy *his* share of reward? The case would be quite different if the same cruel acts had been done by an educated and civilized person, from a mere love of sport. The savage in being reborn would simply take a low place in the scale, by reason of his imperfect moral development; while the *Karma* of the other would be tainted with moral delinquency. . .

"Remember, that we ourselves create our Devachan, as also our Avitchi, while yet on earth, and mostly during the latter days and even moments of our intellectual sentient lives. That feeling which is strongest in us at that supreme hour, when, as in a dream, the events of a long life to their minutest details are marshalled in the greatest order in a few seconds in our vision,* that feeling will become the fashioner of our bliss or woe, the life-principle of our future existence. In the latter we have no substantial being, but only a

---

*That vision takes place when a person is already proclaimed dead. The brain is the last organ that dies.

present and momentary existence, whose duration has no bearing upon, no effect nor relation to its being, which, as every other effect of a transitory cause, will be as fleeting, and in its turn will vanish and cease to be. The real, full remembrance of our lives will come but at the end of the minor cycle—not before. . . . . .

"Unless a man *loves* well, or *hates* well, he need not trouble himself about Devachan; he will be neither in *Devachan* nor Avitchi. 'Nature spews the lukewarm out of her mouth' means only that she annihilates their *personal* Egos (not the Shells, nor yet the 6th Principle) in the Kama Loca and the Devachan. This does not prevent them from being immediately reborn, and if their lives were not very, *very* bad, there is no reason why the eternal Monad should not find the page of that life intact in the Book of Life."

In Kama Loca there is no entity after the separation of the three higher Principles, as described, has taken place. Ordinarily, the interval required for this separation is of brief duration, as compared with the following period in Devachan. But we can easily see that a soul which has lived entirely on the material plane, which has created strong affinities for the grossly physical pleasures of life, will find itself unable to enter the devachanic sleep until these have loosened their hold. When this separation is completed, however, this which was an entity becomes a nonentity. As the Key says:

"Then the kamarupic phantom, remaining bereft of its informing, thinking principle, the higher Manas, and the lower aspect of the latter, the animal intelligence, no longer receiving light from the higher mind, and no longer having a physical brain to work through, collapses. It falls into the state of a frog when certain portions of its brain are taken out by the vivisector. It can think no more, even on the lowest animal plane."

It is in a condition similar to a permanently hypnotized

man. The intelligence which animated it is withdrawn. It is a mere bundle of desires and passions, slowly disin-tegrating, or changing into "skandhas," or effects, wait-ing to attach themselves to the new personality which the Higher Ego enters upon reincarnating. If it float, or is attracted into the aura of a "medium," it may be galvan-ized into apparent consciousness; but this is only apparent. Just as a hypnotized person will obey the will and reflect the thoughts of the hypnotizer, being at the same time utterly unconscious of that which he is doing, so may these "shells," as they are termed, reflect information or opin-ions from the mind of the medium, or of any person pres-ent.

Still there is a Kama Loca entity, proper, which is the "lost soul," to which reference has been made. As we have seen, there may be those who have evolved no possi-bilities of a continued life in Devachan, with its succeed-ing reincarnation. Cultivating none but Kama Loca affin-ities during physical life, the soul finds itself irresistibly drawn downwards to this zone after death, leaving noth-ing to enter Devachan. Its consciousness therefore remains in Kama Loca, an actual, though evil, entity. Such a soul partakes so closely of the earth condition that it is semi- if not wholly, conscious of itself and of its state, especially when it is able to approximate still more closely the earth consciousness through the aura of a medium. This Being realizes that he has nothing before him but the certainty of eternal extinction, and clings to his Kama Loca life with all the tenacity of a drowning man to the handful of earth he has grasped in slipping down the banks of the fatal stream. He it is who haunts "circles," and renews his fading stock of vitality from the life forces of his admiring and unconscious victims.   It is he who materializes; who preaches mock sentimental morality, while compelling his medium to practice exactly the reverse.   Being allied to evil while in the body, he remains an evil force without the body until dissolution overtakes him for the second and last time.

For immortality to be assured, the attraction from the spiritual pole of our being must not be severed, which will be the case if our consciousness does not rise above the fatal equatorial line of materiality when freed from the body by death.   As no soul could reincarnate if there were not in its consciousness enough physical attraction, or longing for sensuous life, to draw it again within material limits when its spiritual tendencies become exhausted in Devachan, so neither can it rise to the permanent and immortal pole of its existence if there is not in its consciousness enough of spiritual attraction to take it above the material planes of being when its body is removed by death.   There is nor can be no "forgiveness" nor "vicarious atonement" in the matter; it is a plain case of cause and effect.   Such a "lost soul" has surrendered itself entirely to the play of material law, and it can but submit to the destruction and disintegration which await all that find expression below the line of permanency and stability.

Remember that analogy holds on all planes; that just as our personal consciousness vibrates during one physical life above and below the line dividing the material from the spiritual, so, in its greater cycle, the true man, or Reincarnating Ego, is also vibrating between these poles—each incarnation being but a single vibration.   Now a personality drags it towards the material pole; now another elevates it far in the direction of the spiritual. And just as the personality has in its vibrations but one end in view—the union with its Higher Ego—so this Higher Ego has in its reincarnating vibrations the sole object of uniting with its Higher Self, or with the Divine Consciousness of Atma-Buddhi. This union of the Higher Ego with its Higher Self is one aspect of Nirvana, and this is why an Adept attains Nirvana during life. His personal consciousness has united itself to his Higher Ego, and this Higher Ego, united to the Higher Self, enables him to thus experience temporarily Nirvanic consciousness.

Of Nirvana, we of undeveloped spiritual perception can of necessity know but very little. It is only to correct popular misconception that it is referred to here at all. Able Sanscrit scholars have defined it as "annihilation of consciousness." This is because Western thought has become so infected with materialism that it recognizes only material or personal consciousness. This is annihilated; and in its annihilation we find supreme happiness, for it enables us to attain to the immortality of true spiritual consciousness.

In the non-recognition of spiritual consciousness, or consciousness unlimited by the illusions of matter, lies the source of the Western misapprehension of the term "Nirvana." As the human consciousness rises more and more toward the spiritual pole of its being, it becomes, *pari passu*, less limited by matter, with its darkness and grossness, and finds its area of perception continuously widening, until, upon reaching Nirvana, it has become one with the Whole. It has not, by any means, lost its individuality, but its consciousness has become so marvelously widened that it embraces the whole of manifested nature.

If this glorious enlargement of perception and consciousness, until nature has no further secrets hidden from
our enlightened senses, can be called annihilation, then
is our human consciousness annihilated; not otherwise.
There is an infinity of difference between the annihilation
of our puerile personal consciousness, and CONSCIOUS
rest in Omniscience.

All these states—Nirvana, Kama Loca, and Devachan—
have no hard and fast lines which separate them from
each other.   On the contrary, each is subdivided into an
infinity of minor planes, the upper of which pass by inap-
preciable gradations into the next succeeding ones.
Therefore Devachan in nowise resembles the Christian's
heaven in its dreary sameness, nor does Kama Loca
plunge all into the one pit of flaming brimstone.   In like
manner, Nirvana, while interchaining its lower planes
with the upper of Devachan, passes from thence through
such an innumerable succession of higher zones that we
find a variety of definitions of it given, and all correct from
the point of view taken.   Thus, in the Secret Doctrine and
other writings of Madame Blavatsky, we find Nirvana
spoken of as a synonym for the laya state, or " that of the
dissociation of all substances merged after a life cycle into
their original condition of latency."   Again, it is stated
that as Devachan is a state of rest between two lives, in
like manner Nirvana is a state of rest intervening between
two world chains.   As this would imply the dissociation
of matter, it would agree with the preceding definition,
while as each world chain includes almost an infinity of
conscious progress, so the Nirvana preceding and following any one of them would differ widely in its degree of
consciousness, while still answering to the definition.

In another reference it is stated that Buddhists teach that only "two things are objectively eternal—Nirvana and Akasa," which again throws a side light, so to speak, upon this state. Farther on, we are told that a Nirvanee can not return during the manvantara to which he belongs, which, as his consciousness has become dissociated from matter as we know it, again agrees with the first definition. Again, in the "Voice of the Silence," we are told that Nirvana—its lower planes, no doubt, being meant—is a plane of exalted spiritual selfishness, if struggled for and obtained while the great mass of one's fellowmen are still suffering in the bonds of matter. Thus it is taught in India that Buddha and several of his Arhats refused to enter Nirvana, after having won the right to it; but out of their great compassion for mankind remain as Nirmanakayas in order to help its upward progress.

Returning to the question of annihilation in Nirvana, Madame Blavatsky, in the Secret Doctrine, says:

"To see in Nirvana annihilation amounts to saying of a man plunged in sound, dreamless sleep—one that leaves no impression on the physical memory and brain, because the sleeper's Higher Self is in its original state of Absolute Consciousness during these hours—that he, too, is annilated. The latter simile answers to only one side of the question—the most material; since reabsorption is by no means such a dreamless sleep, but, on the contrary, absolute existence, an unconditioned unity, or a state to describe which human language is absolutely and hopelessly inadequate. Nor is the individuality, nor even the essence of the personality, if any be left behind, lost because reabsorbed. For however limitless from a human standpoint the paranirvanic state, it has yet a limit in eternity. Once reached, the same monad will re-emerge therefrom, as a still higher being, on a far higher plan, to recommence its cycle of perfected activity. The human mind cannot in its present stage of development transcend, scarcely reach, this plane of thought. It totters here on the brink of incomprehensible absoluteness and eternity."

In conclusion, it will become apparent from this portion of our study that we create the conditions which control our Post-mortem states while we are yet within the physical body; that life in and out of the body pursues its eternal course in obedience to the absolute law of cause and effect, to which it forms no exception; and that therefore man can not enter upon a wiser course of study than that which relates to his own nature, origin and destiny. The object of our most strenuous exertions ought to be to transfer our consciousness from the impermanent to the permanent; from the mortal, to the immortal. So long as our personal consciousness is limited to sensuous planes, so long must the subjective cycles of our existence be passed in an unconscious, sleep-like condition, with the possibility of perishing at any time by being drawn permanently within the attraction of matter. Or it might be caught by some cataclysmic, physical change in one of these unconscious subjective states, and eons of ages elapse before another opportunity be afforded for such an undeveloped Ego to again take up the evolution of its consciousness. Suppose our world went into Pralaya before certain souls had attained to true, or spiritual self-consciousness. During this Pralaya there would be an universal Nirvana for the whole of humanity, owing to the dissociation of matter—a period of world rest, analogous to the night's rest between days, or the devachanic between lives. But such undeveloped souls would have to enter Nirvana as they now do Devachan, unconscious, except for this false, sleep-like consciousness, which must soon exhaust its material, even if it can utilize it here at all;

and then what? There is no more an earth fitted for them to continue their efforts awaiting the termination of the devachanic sleep, and they must remain unconscious during the whole sweep of Nirvanic duration. Hear the same Teacher:*

" But there is a great difference between conscious and unconscious being. The condition of Paranirvana without Paramartha, the self-analyzing consciousness, is no bliss, but simply extinction (for seven eternities). Thus an iron ball placed under the scorching rays of the sun will get heated through, but will not appreciate the warmth, while man will. It is only with a mind clear and undarkened by personality, and the assimilation of the merit of manifold existence devoted to being in its collectivity (the whole living and sentient universe), that one gets rid of personal existence, merging into and becoming one with the Absolute, and continuing in full possession of Paramartha."†

---

*Secret Doctrine.

†Paramartha—Self-consciousness, without which, as stated, even Nirvana is simply extinction while it endures.

CHAPTER XI.

HYPNOTISM AND THE HUMAN SOUL.

THE relation of the soul to the body can, in certain aspects, be made clearer by a study of the phenomena of Hypnotism than, perhaps, by any other method. Most, if not all, of these can only be explained by admitting the presence and superior powers of a center of consciousness, or soul, which is actually limited in its conscious manifestations by the sense organs instead of being helped by them.

As bases from whence to survey the field of hypnotic phenomena, we must return to the scientific and self-evident postulates of a Unit of Consciousness, and the Compound Nature of Man.

By a unit is meant a center of consciousness, which, like the mathematical point, excludes from its conception all measures of time or space. Such centers are infinite in number as potentialities; while as potencies, actively ascending the spiral of evolution, they embrace all degrees from the center of consciousness present and potent in an "atom" to that of the highest Dhyani-Buddhi, or "god." By an atom is not meant the materialistic definition of this. There is no attempt at dividing matter until it is presumably incapable of further division, and then setting up this hypothetical infinitesimal "element" as a measure of both the material and the spiritual worlds, as science would fain do. Holding that "the Universe is worked and guided from within outwards,"* and that as

*Secret Doctrine, Vol. 1, p. 274.

we pass from the outer, material phenomena to the inner, spiritual noumena, matter becomes not less and less in the size or extension of its particles, but more and more ethereal and homogeneous in its essence, Theosophy defines an atom as the seventh or guiding principle of the first differentiation of the homogeneity of the plane above ours toward the heterogeneity of this material plane.

But this center of consciousness, although regarded as unity, still presents that Trinity in Unity which accompanies all conceptions of the One Absolute. As this, though one and indivisible, is yet matter, or substance; force, or motion; and consciousness, or ideation—so the unit of consciousness we term human—which is only that of an atom extended by countless accretions of material expressions and experiences—presents the triple aspects of Thought, Will, and Feeling. It is with the second of these, or Will, that a study of hypnotism must largely deal.

But what *is* the Will? Locke* declares that:

"That power which the mind has to order the consideration of an idea, or the forbearing to consider it, or to prefer the motion of any part of the body or its rest, and *vice versa*, in any particular instance, is that which we call the will. It signifies nothing but the power to prefer or choose, and thought determines it. Desire and will are two distinct acts, and desire determines the will."

Lewes† says, by implication, that the Will is only the play of molecular forces, under the unconscious law of cause and effect. Upham‡ regards the Will as the Understanding or Ideation in action—the active aspect of Consciousness. Bain§ holds that the Will is that power in Consciousness which controls spontaneous ideation, or

---

*Essay on the Human Understanding.   ‡Mental Philosophy.
†Philosophy of Life and Mind.   §Senses and Intellect.

ideation which naturally arises in the course of evolution through the reaction between the subject and its environment.

But see the prince of modern Agnosticism, Herbert Spencer,* seize the fiery Fohat of the Occultist and drag him, a helpless captive, at the wheel of his materialistic chariot. He writes:

"When automatic actions become so involved, so varied in kind, and severally so infrequent as no longer to be performed with unhesitating precision—when after the reception of one of the more complex impressions, the appropriate motor changes become nascent, but are prevented from passing into immediate action by the antagonism of certain other nascent motor changes, appropriate to some nearly allied impression; there is constituted a state of consciousness which, when it finally issues into action, displays what we term volition. We have a conflict between two sets of ideal motor changes which severally tend to become real, and this passing of an ideal motor change into a real one we distinguish as Will. Thus the cessation of automatic action and the dawn of volition are one and the same thing."

In other words, the mighty, creative volitions of a Shakespeare, a Gœthe, a Dante, a Bacon, an Edison, a Newton, a Harvey, a Galileo, a Kant, a Hegel, or even Spencer's own speculations, are merely the fortuitous emergence of one set of "nascent," unconscious motor changes slightly in advance of other equally unconscious ones, which blind chance has thus caused to be lost to the world forever ! What a relief to feel and, indeed, know, by "scientific authority," that the horrible visions of Dante were not deliberately evoked, but were enabled to "issue into action" in advance of a milder set, perchance by

*Principles of Pscyhology.

the unconscious assistance of a very badly digested din-
ner !   An Occultist would declare that the very ability to
choose even the subject of our thoughts indicates an inherent power in consciousness which no fortuitous combination of material molecules could ever evoke, though all
eternity were granted it in which to exert its "blind force."
The stream cannot rise higher than its source; the effect
can not exceed its cause; and Will, manifesting as an aspect and power of Consciousness on this material, phenomenal plane, must have its origin and cause in that
larger, Cosmic, noumenal plane—the Force-Aspect of the
Absolute.

Will, then, from a Theosophic standpoint, is Desire in
action guided by Ideation, which latter again is the active
aspect of Consciousness, or Consciousness in action.   In
man, Will is one aspect of the center of consciousness, or
Ray, which takes its source directly in the Absolute or
Unknowable, and around which has evolved the feeling of
"I am I" through accretions of material experiences and
expressions in the manner pointed out in the chapter
upon the Individualization of the Soul.   This center,
though a unity in essence, is a trinity in aspect, and because of this unity of base, all three aspects merge into
one another, or, rather, into that unity of which they are
the phenomenal expression.   Will selects the subject of
Thought; yet Thought, again, will so modify the Will that
we find ourselves desiring or willing that which before we
compelled ourselves to think it desirable was repugnant to
us.   Feeling, also, particularly in its lowest aspect of
emotion, will modify both Thought and Will, and be in
turn itself modified and transmuted by them.

This brings us to the standpoint from which we have to

examine hypnotism, and all psychic or mental phenomena. Will, as one aspect, function, or power of Consciousness, is struggling to evolve its potencies, now benumbed and paralyzed by its primal "fall" into matter.
Thought and Feeling are likewise in the thralldom of the
flesh, and are also in the course of an evolutionary effort
to find their ultimate state of full and free expression.
To perfect man, all three aspects of Consciousness must
be rounded out or developed symmetrically. In the
natural course of evolution, emotion emerges first, and we
see in the limitations of the animal kingdom the effect of
asymmetry in the evolution of only one aspect of Consciousness. As we have seen in the study of the Evolution of the Soul, it is the incarnation in human-animal
forms of Egos which have evolved other aspects of consciousness in other worlds which causes the great and
otherwise inexplicable hiatus in the evolutionary process—
the missing link which so puzzles and confounds the Dar-
winians. Because of this asymmetry in evolution, men
have will power and mental energy developed in various
degrees of feebleness, and in dissimilar directions. This
accounts for the ability of one will to control another,
through superior development along some particular line.
This line may be in the direction of evil quite as often as
in that of good; and in the case of professional hypnotizers
it is almost always by the strong development of some
selfish trait of the character that they are enabled to over-
power those who are purer or even more intellectual than
they. It is becoming strong in evil which is the origin of
the power of the Black Magician.

Now, to the Theosophist, the development of the Will
does not mean the empty abstraction which it conveys to

the scientist. It is the becoming potent of a conscious force, having its own ratio of vibration, and using a material vehicle in a manner exactly corresponding to force on the material plane. Hence, when a hypnotizer compels another to obey his will, he has subjected him to an actual force conveyed by a vehicle of matter quite as certainly as has the prize-fighter when he "knocks out" his helpless antagonist. There are no empty abstractions or immaterial agents for a student of Theosophy, however much his scientific brother may be compelled to resort to them. The hypnotizer has directed a part of his own "nerve fluid" upon and into the nervous system of his victim, where it remains an actual force, establishing new and modifying centers of vibration, which act in obedience to the ideation which accompanied it. There has been an actual transfer of substance, force, and consciousness—a setting up of new conscious centers in a manner exactly analogous to the new centers of physical or molecular vibrations which are the result of the taking into the system of physical remedies or "medicines." No scientist nor physician has ever offered a rational explanation of the methods by which physical remedies act. But to the Theosophist who recognizes vibratory motion as the universally present Force-Aspect of the Causeless Cause, the reason is plain. Such physical molecules establish innumerable centers of vibratory motion, which modify the vibrations of the molcules in the physiological or pathological cells of the body, according as their ratios of vibration are multiples or "chords" of these. The "selective affinity" of the physiological empiricist in explaining the action of drugs is but a formula for expressing a law of harmonic vibrations of whose real action he is quite ignorant. In like manner the will of the hypnotizer establishes innumerable force centers which prevent the consciousness of the Ego from controlling its own sense organs. It is the same kind of process as that which takes place when the vibratory centers set up by chloroform or morphine interpose actual physical obstacles between the soul and its sense organs through the "affinity" between their vibratory ratios and those of the brain molecules.

Of course, scientists will deny this. The very name "hypnotism" had its origin in this denial. The Paris Academy had solemnly "sat" upon the phenomena exhibited by Mesmer, and had pronounced them pure delusions. But the ghost refused to remain laid at their bidding, and so Braid, in the 'thirties of this century, undertook to exorcise it anew. Being honest and earnest, he was soon compelled to admit the reality of the phenomena of Mesmerism, but denied *in toto* that the will of another had anything to do with their production. According to his theory, the phenomena were entirely self-induced, and the will of the operator no further shares than to merely "suggest" them to the subject, who thereupon hypnotized or mesmerized himself.

Braid's assumption was eminently consistent with materialistic teachings; for if the will were merely a function of matter in a state of molecular vibration, and had no power of action outside the molecular environment which created it, then nothing could pass from the hypnotizer to the hypnotized, who must, therefore, be the sole factor in the phenomena. Proceeding upon this assumption, he re-named these "hypnotism," or the science of the sleep-like states; from *hypnos*, sleep. This name has been retained by science, notwithstanding that the theory

of Braid, upon which it was based, has been entirely dis-
proven by later scientific invest'gations—notably those
conducted by members of the same Academy which had
a few years preceding pronounced Mesmerism an hallucination, or worse. As there are psychic and subjective
states which can be self-induced without-the interference
of any exterior will, it would seem proper to limit the
name, "hypnotism," to these self-induced states; reserving
Mesmerism for those which Mesmer, in modern times at
least, first demonstrated. However, that is as science
may elect. Theosophy retains both terms; calling those
phenomena hypnotic which emanate from or are originated
in the plane of selfishness or Kama, and those mesmeric
which proceed from the higher or Manasic plane. One is
Black, the other White, magic. These differ in their manner of production, in the material vehicles which they
employ, and in other ways, which will be pointed out
later. It will thus be seen how important a bearing the
recognition of a Unit, or center of human consciousness,
manifesting through the several vehicles composing the
Septenary nature of man, has upon the proper understanding of the phenomena of hypnotism and Mesmerism,
as well as various allied states, such as somnambulism,
trance, thought-reading, clairvoyance, etc. A non-
recognition of the one Unit, functioning differently in differing vehicles or bases, has caused the most curious speculations among the observers of these phenomena. For
with every grade of depth in the hypnotic process such
new and unsuspected mental powers made their appearance that it seemed the startling fact that there were several "selves" buried in the personality, distinct and dis-
tinguishable from the one we recognize, was distinctly

pointed out.   In fact, as the number of these apparently
separate persons exhumed out of one body by hypnosis
seemed practically unlimited, the deduction fairly followed
that as consciousness could be thus split into a series of
illusionary personalities there was no real conscious entity, or human soul, but only states of consciousness depending upon the particular form of " molecular activity."
Still, there were awkward facts for the "molecular activity"
theory to account for.   Although the enlightened and
philosophic consciousness buried in a stupid peasant's
body refused to believe itself identical with the peasant,
still it remembered and knew all about the peasant's life
and mental capacities, thus showing a unifying something
at the basis of consciousness.   And this followed through
all the separate persons which were, apparently, exhumed
out of the one Personality.   Each knew and remembered
all about those below it, while remaining profoundly
ignorant of any above.

At this perplexing stage, Theosophy points out the solution of the mystery.   The one Unit and Center of
Consciousness on the physical plane unifies and connotes
the various mental states pertaining to matter into our
ordinary consciousness;   the waking, willing, thinking,
feeling " I am I."   But this same center of consciousness
can and does—under proper conditions—experience the
feeling of " I am I" on other planes, and in other states
of matter.   Passing to the lower astral plane during the
waking-sleeping state, it recognizes itself as quite a distinct
person from the waking one;   capable of flying, leaping,
and many things then impossible.   If it could be now
told that it was the waking self, it would naturally deny
this, although all the time there would be the consciousness that there was such a person in existence.

Similarly, on planes as much higher than the waking as this is lower, it would no doubt be disinclined to believe itself the same limited, stupid person it is when its spiritual powers are so dulled and obscured by matter.

Thus we find that all the varied phenomena of mesmeric, hypnotic, clairvoyant, magnetic—in short, all normal or abnormal mental states are simply the one consciousness, functioning now through this vehicle, now through that. In Mesmerism and hypnotism, as commonly understood, it is the will of another which compels the "I am I" center of consciousness to abandon its ordinary physical vehicles and retire to others. In self-hypnosis, such as is done by all so-called "mediums" when they really get into the trance state, exactly the same thing occurs under the force of their own will. And these self-induced states may also be divided into the mesmeric and hypnotic, according as the plane upon which the hypnotizer habitually lives is selfish or unselfish, kamic or manasic.

But merely to say that the Will of another causes these hypnotic conditions only leaves the matter where we found it; especially if we regard the Will as the immaterial non-entity of materialism. For this reason, this study was preceded by an inquiry as to the nature and functions of the Will. We have seen that in willing there is an actual transfer of substance as the vehicle of force, and both these under the guidance of Consciousness in its active aspect of Ideation. The Cosmic Will is known in Occultism as Fohat, and the human will is but one of its countless correlations. All willing, from the fohatic to the human, is a controlling—or attempting to control or direct—that primary Force or Motion, the Force-Aspect of the Causeless Cause. Therefore, hypnotism is an attempt, by means of the will of the hypnotizer, to modify or control that molecular motion which enables consciousness to manifest in the organism of another being.

The very first step in hypnotism or Mesmerism, then, is to modify the rate of vibration in the subject sought to be influenced until it becomes identical with, or a ratio of, our own. As all life and consciousness manifest through motion, it will be seen how necessary that the vibration in any two subjects sought to be related in the intimacy of the hypnotic states should be in proportion, or harmonious. They may not be identical, but they must stand in the relation of harmonic chords to each other—unless the one completely replaces the other. This is the solution of the mystery of the production of the hypnotic state by gazing at bright objects, by musical or sudden sounds, etc. In gazing fixedly at a bright object, with the will directed to that end, the point in the human brain which correlates spiritual motion or intelligence with the material plane assumes a rate or ratio of vibration identical with the object so gazed at, and the hypnotized body falls into a similar if not identical state of consciousness. The center of consciousness, being thus compelled to abandon its *point d'appui* with its material frame, either remains in a dormant condition or functions through one of its more subtle vehicles, or " bodies." In case of self-hypnosis, as in mediums or trance seers, the "I am I" usually establishes itself upon the plane of matter just above the physical, known in Theosophy as the astral, and is there subject to all the hallucinations and illusions which attend upon this condition, and of which we can form a very good idea by its close identity with the ordi-

nary dreaming state. In hypnosis by another, with or
without the subject's acquiescence, the center of consciousness is forced to abandon its hold upon the body first of
all, which assumes the "lethargic" condition of Charcot
and his school. The hypnotizer's will then takes complete possession, and the subject obeys the slightest suggestion, either spoken or mental, relating to the material
plane, such as leaping, dancing, assuming grotesque or
absurd positions, tasting the same object as sweet on
one side of the tongue and bitter on the other, seeing reflections in pasteboard mirrors, or pictures upon blank
cards. Rigidity, or tetanus of the muscles, also occurs, and
a thousand-and-one other acts, over which scientists have
been so puzzled, not having the key. This key is, that
every one of these acts, from tetanus to double tasting or
picture-seeing where none exist, are pure "suggestions,"
many of which are unconsciously made by the hypnotizer.
He has possession of the physical brain of his subject to
an extent of which he is little aware, and it responds to
his most subtle, unworded thought. "Suggestion" is only
the obedience by the subject's body and brain to the same
will currents and finer forces by means of which he gov-
erns his own body and mind; and could not take place,
even in ordinary, unhypnotic suggestions, if the center of
consciousness had not relaxed, to a certain degree at least,
its hold upon its own body. In lethargic hypnosis this
hold is loosened until it amounts to a practical abandonment of its tenement.

But this center of consciousness can not be annihilated.
Driven from its physical habitation, it will, under a more
determined effort of the hypnotizer, or under the impetus
of the self-hypnotizer's will, reappear, functioning in more

and more ethereal bases, or "Principles," until it finally retreats, or is driven to a point where the will of the hypnotizer, no matter how powerful, can no longer control it. This may be called the Noetic or Manasic point, as distinguished from the lower, or psychic states. There are many sub-stages before this point of freedom is reached, in which this Center, using bases more and more spiritualized, displays apparently more and more "supernatural" powers, which are only those appropriate to these planes of materiality. In all of them the subject is influenced and controlled to a greater or lesser degree by the will of the hypnotizer, and all opinions, ideas and knowledge modified and measured by his. This, again, is the key to that large class of phenomena just a step above those of which we have spoken, and which may be termed psychic, as those below them were termed physical, and those above Noetic or Manasic.

It is in this psychic realm that almost all of the so-called "spiritual" manifestations find their *habitat*, when these display any intelligence at all. This is the home of "seers" and "clairvoyants," of fakirs and fortune-tellers. For he who can by self-hypnosis, or by the aid of another, establish his consciousness upon this psychic plane, will find himself possessed of powers which are just as natural here as ordinary sight and hearing are on the physical. One of the most important of these is the ability to sense thought without its having been materialized in words. This is known as "mind reading," and all those who reach this plane can do this to a greater or lesser degree. Direct perception, without the intervention at least of the physical senses, appears upon the higher of these psychic or somnambulic planes, as is shown in cases where hypnotized subjects have correctly diagnosed and located physical ailments, unsuspected before their pointing them out, and verified by subsequent *post-mortem* examinations. These diagnoses, however, are strictly limited upon this psychic plane to self-diagnosis, or at least have little or no value if they are attempted to be made upon another person. Wonderful as many of the feats done by psychics are, they still fall under the classification of mind-reading, for any information which they give must, to be accurate, already exist in the mind of some one present. Thus one of the most noted, the celebrated Alexis, failed completely to read an unopened letter, the contents of which were unknown to his interlocutor, although he correctly described the personal appearance and surroundings of the sender, which were known. Had the contents been subjected to even a single reading, Alexis would no doubt have read the letter correctly, although his interlocutor could not have repeated it from memory, which shows how complete a picture of all the acts and thoughts of our life is recorded upon the physical tablets of the brain—an open book to whomever has the power to read. It also indicates how marvelously mental powers are quickened when the mind no longer functions through its lowest or molecular vehicle.

But far above all these psychic states lies the domain of true Mesmerism, with a class of phenomena peculiarly its own, and which are but very seldom brought to view by the ordinary peripatetic, or even the " scientific," hypnotizer. Indeed, it is this plane which the hypnotizer seeks to avoid, because, as he complains, his subject "gets beyond his control," Yet it is this very point which divides White from Black Magic; and all who stop short of it through ignorance or fear may know the class to which they belong. The very vibrations of the hypnotic state pertain to a lower plane of matter. They are *Molecular*, and can be produced by attuning the consciousness to molecular vibration, such as gazing at bright objects, etc., as pointed out above. The Mesmeric, Noetic, or Manasic vibrations are *Atomic*, and proceed from a much higher plane, and in an exactly opposite direction. The vibrations in hypnotism pass from without within; those of Mesmerism from within without, in harmony with the law of evolution. The one is on the plane of Kama, or selfish desire, and is destructive in its nature; the other on that of Manas, unselfishness, and is creative, life-giving, Cosmic Magnetism. As pointed out by Wm. Q. Judge,* "the process going on in hypnotism is the contraction of the cells of the body and the brain from the periphery to the center. This is actually a phenemenon of death, and is, the opposite of the mesmeric effect. Magnetism by human influence starts from within and proceeds to the outer surface, thus, exhibiting a phenomenon of life the very opposite of hypnotism." If we remember that the occult definition of an atom is the seventh or conscious principle of a molecule, we can see that the play of the one is on the plane of blind, the other of intelligent, force, respectively. This is why the action of Mesmerism is curative and helpful in its nature. It is acting in harmony with nature's processes; it is the evolution from within without, under which law the whole Universe exists.

The phenomena of Mesmerism, or, more properly,

---

*Hypnotism and Theosophy.

Magnetism, are of a nature we might anticipate from the close union of the soul with the source of all its powers, the Higher Ego. They are prophetic, intuitional, universal. As on the higher planes of the psychic states, the soul seems to contact and sense material things without the intervention of the physical senses, so upon this it arrives directly at intellectual truths, without the aids of reasoning or ratiocinative processes. Prophecies of the death of their body, as well as future events on the material plane, are common to somnambulists who have reached this condition, although these are of the very lowest of mesmeric powers. Prophetic dreams fall under this head, as they are simply the Higher Ego functioning upon its own proper plane, and a glimpse of whose knowledge has been impressed upon the brain cells of the personality. Indeed, one great and deep distinction between the hypnotic and mesmeric states is that the former requires that the Ego should be made unconscious on the material plane before its phenomena can fully and freely issue, while mesmeric effects can be produced quite independently of the unconsciousness and destruction of the Will by any of the hypnotic adjuncts. The mesmeric phenomena proceed from the higher, inner planes, and can and do cause an influx of life, strength, and vigor into the physical system of the mesmerized subject while he is in the full possession of all his ordinary mental powers, and quite unconscious that any such process is taking place. Indeed, this unconsciousness is often mutual; neither the giver nor receiver being aware of what is taking place, or, in the case of Mental and Christian Science, not knowing how or why they cure disease when this follows upon their "treatments." It is simply the transfer of their own vital, electric, atomic magnetism, taking place under the passive aspect of the will, or Desire. Its principal agent is the eye, usually assisted by "passes," in contradistinction to the crystal gazing, or other physical methods, of hypnotism. The actual *modus operandi* of the two processes necessary in the production of Mesmerism and hypnotism have been nicely distinguished by Madame Blavatsky. She writes:*

"When the first method (Braid's) is used, no electro-psychic, or even electro-physical currents are at work, but simply the mechanical, molecular vibrations of the metal or crystal gazed at by the subject. It is the eye—the most occult organ of all on the superficies of our body—which, by serving as a medium between that bit of metal or crystal and the brain, attunes the molecular vibrations of the nervous centers of the latter into unison (*i. e.*, equality in the number of their respective oscillations) with the vibrations of the bright object held. And it is this unison which produces the hypnotic state. But, in the second case, the right name for hypnotism would certainly be 'animal magnetism,' or that so much derided term, Mesmerism. For, in the hypnotization by preliminary passes, it is the human will —whether conscious or otherwise—of the operator himself that acts upon the nervous system of the patient. And it is again through the vibrations—only atomic, not molecular—produced by that act of energy called WILL in the ether of space (therefore on quite a different plane) that the super-hypnotic (*i. e.*, 'suggestion,' etc.,) is induced. For those which we call will-vibrations and their aura are absolutely distinct from the vibrations produced by the simple mechanical molecular motion, the two acting on separate degrees of the cosmo-terrestrial planes."

These statements, again, will be derided by so-called "science." With them "suggestion"—by which is meant, according to Dr. Bjornstrom,† "every operation which in

---

a living being causes some involuntary effect, the impulse
to which passes through the intellect"—covers the whole
of this *terra incognita*. How the idea that she is hypnotized and unable to move is "impulsed" through the intellect of a hen, from the point of whose bill a chalk line
is drawn upon the ground in front of her, we leave for
some learned "Psychical Research Society" to investigate;
the subject may be upon its intellectual level. In fact,
"suggestion," as accounting for hypnotism upon the
theory of ideas set up in the subject, entirely breaks down
before the facts of the hypnosis of animals. Let a man
stand in front of a hungry lion and "suggest" to him that
he is not hungry, and he will presently find himself within
the stomach of the beast; while, if he can catch the eye,
and has the courage and knowledge to attune its vibrations to his own, he need not fear the most ferocious denizen of the forest. This is the secret of the Rareys and
lion-tamers, which they unconsciously exercise; and,
indeed, it is the secret of that "dominion over every beast
of the earth" which has enabled man to make them his
unwilling subjects from the day that he first appreciated
the strength of his human will.

From all of the preceding, it will be gathered that
Theosophists look with no friendly eye upon the practice
of hypnotism, except under the most strict legal and
moral supervision. The dangers are many, and self
evident. If the very walls and stones preserve a record
of shadows cast across them, which even science admits,
how much more lasting the impression produced upon the
sensitive brain structure by the deliberate and forcible
impress of the will of another. It is a matter of grave
doubt whether the hypnotized, after a thorough hypnosis,

ever regain perfectly free will and entirely normal consciousness.   Certain well-verified phenomena would indicate the reverse.   For example: It is related of a well known hypnotizer—then classed as a "miracle" worker, or magnetic healer—that he once removed a neuralgia, of long standing, from the arm of a certain sufferer, who thereupon returned to his own country.   After some years of perfect freedom, the pain suddenly returned one day, with all its former intensity.   Inquiry revealed the startling fact that at the very hour in which it did so the magnetizer had died.

Quite as suggestive is the case, vouched for by several hypnotizers, where the sleeping subject was ordered to do a certain act at some designated interval after he was awakened.   The hypnosis was then removed, and the subject to all appearances widely awake;—quite free to think and act as he pleased.   Yet, when the time arrived at which he was commanded to do it, he obeyed as implicitly as though he were yet completely hypnotized.   But, though acting with apparently full consciousness and knowledge of what he did, he denied immediately afterward that he had performed any such action at all, and could not be convinced to the contrary.   This experiment, verified by many similar ones, showed plainly that, though apparently awake, as far as human observation could detect, the subject was not so fully and completely, and that a portion of his normal consciousness was entirely suppressed and under the subjugation of the will of another.

From a criminal standpoint, also, these suggestions obeyed after long intervals of apparently complete self-control have a most important bearing.   Suggestions have been carried out down to the most minute, trifling detail after even a year had elapsed since the hypnosis. It is easy to see how a hypnotizer could cause any crime which avarice or revenge might dictate to be accomplished without its being possible to connect him legally with that for which he is morally responsible.

Again, a suggestion often, if not always, acts like a physical stimulus in a dream, as when a drop of water on the face has caused the dramatization of a whole sequence of thunder-storm, shipwreck, etc., by the dreamer. Similarly, a seemingly simple suggestion may set up a train of desires, utterly out of proportion to the primary impulse, as a city may be destroyed by the accidental lighting of a match. Thus, in one instance* it was suggested to the subject that she desired some cherries. Instead of passing off when awakened this desire increased in intensity, and was only satisfied by the purchase of some the next day.

It is now, also, after a stormy denial on the part of science, universally admitted that hypnotism can be produced from a distance, without the subject knowing it, against his will, and even during sleep. In all these instances so far recorded there has been a magnetic *rapport* established by a submission to hypnosis before these disputed phenomena could be accomplished, which only adds strength to the view that the hypnotized is never free from the will of the hypnotizer again, the *rapport* simply meaning in these cases a state of partial hypnosis. It also emphasizes the fact that one ought to submit to any torture rather than be hypnotized, and that he had far better "experiment" with the most deadly physical

---

*Bjornstrom, *loc. cit.*

poisons than with this equally deadly moral one.   There is no apparent reason why all of these terrible powers for evil could not be exercised upon any one by a Black Magician, sufficiently versed in his art.   And there is no question that a pursuit of the study together with a practice of hypnotism will ultimately end in Black magic for all its lay practitioners.   The distinction between Black and White Magic is in MOTIVE only; the forces used are the same.   There must be a perfect and complete altruism, an utter abandonment of self, before we can rise to the planes of Mesmerism and White magic.   The sweetest, purest, most ethereal " Christian Scientist" who accepts a fee for her "denial" that her patient is ill or her affirmation that he is well, has taken the first step on the declivity which will sooner or later lead to the awful precipices of the Black Magician, from which there is no escape; for there is the element of self, no matter how seemingly justifiable, which will prove the germ that will ultimately poison her whole being.   The operations of most "healers" have this in common with White Magic and Mesmerism, that their "suggestions" are made with the subject in full possession of all his mental faculties and consciousness, and are not accompanied with that soul-tainting, will-destroying, obsessing vampirism of the hypnotic "sleep."   It is true that the latter may be apparently justified in order to overcome a peculiarly stubborn will or vicious habit, but where it is resorted to, the motive ought to be as pure as the snow upon the hights of the Himalayas.

This brings us to the consideration of the question as to the extent to which hypnotism may be justifiably practiced.   Its field would seem to be limited to attempts to cure disease, and to overcome bad habits, and, in selecting cases, the nicest discrimination, guided by considerations pointed out, must ·be used. Madame Blavatsky,* whose knowledge of occult subjects far exceeded that of any living writer, defines its legitimate uses and points out some of its abuses thus: .

"Hypnotic suggestion may cure forever, and .it may not. If Karmic, diseases will only be postponed, and return in ·some other form, not necessarily of disease, but as a punitive evil of another sort. It is always right to try and alleviate suffering whenever we can, and to do our best for it. Thought is more, powerful than speech in cases of a real subjugation of the will of the patient to that of his operator. But, on the other hand, unless the suggestion made is for the good only of the subject, and entirely free from any selfish motive, a suggestion by thought is an action of Black Magic still more pregnant with evil consequences than a spoken suggestion. It is always wrong and unlawful to deprive a man of his free will, unless for his own or society's good, and even the former has to be done with great discrimination. Occultism regards all such promiscuous attempts as Black Magic and sorcery, whether conscious or otherwise. As to whether it is wise to hypnotize a patient out of a vicious habit, such as drinking or lying, it is an act of charity and kindness, and this is next to wisdom. For, although the dropping of his vicious habits will add nothing to his good Karma (which it would had ·his efforts to reform been personal, of his own free will, and necesitating a great mental and physical struggle), still a successful 'suggestion' prevents him from generating more bad Karma, and adding con-stantly to the previous record of his transgressing."

In regard to the *modus operandi* of " faith" healing, she further says:

"Imagination is a potent help in every event of our lives. Imag-ination acts on faith, and both are the draughtsmen who prepare the

---

sketches for will to engrave, more or less deeply, on the rocks of obstacles and opposition with which the path of life is strewn. Says Paracelsus, 'Faith must confirm the imagination, for faith establishes the will. Determined will is the beginning of all magical operations. It is because men do not perfectly imagine and believe the result that the arts (of magic) are uncertain while they might be pefectly certain.' This is all the secret. Half, if not two-thirds, of all our ailings and diseases are the fruit of our imagination and fears. Destroy the latter and give another bent to the former, and nature will do the rest. There is nothing injurious or sinful in the methods, *per se*. They turn to harm only when belief in his power becomes too arrogant and marked in the faith healer, and when he thinks he can will away such diseases as need, if they are to be removed at all, the immediate help of expert surgeons and physicians.''

But, perhaps, the chief reason for abstaining from the practice of hypnotism, except in extreme cases, and under the restrictions pointed out, is our blind ignorance of the finer forces of nature which we are evoking. Thus, it happened to the writer to find that a subject, whom he had hypnotized merely as a pleasant evening's entertainment, appeared to become afterward a kind of reflector of his (the writer's) mental states and ideas. Let the writer be thinking of a subject, and his patient would allude to it; let him mentally hum a song, and he would be startled by hearing his unconscious serf immediately vocalizing it, etc., and all this with no desire or thought on the writer's part that this should follow.

A paragraph which went the rounds of the press some time since is very instructive in this connection. It is to the effect that a certain Spaniard, named Perez, arriving at Mier, Mexico, was immediately made the recipient of gifts of a varied character from people to whom he was a perfect stranger. Some of these were silly, as when the waiter removed all the bottles of wine from the other guests, and transferred them to the tables of Perez. Being threatened with violence, and called upon to explain, Perez admitted that he was a trained and marvelously. proficient hypnotizer, which had become such a passion that he could not resist practicing his gift upon those about him. But it is evident from the account given that Perez often hypnotized people without himself being aware of it. And here we have a key to the states of consciousness portrayed in " Mr. Jekyll and Mr. Hyde," as also to that delineated by one who, we have many reasons for believing, founded his occult stories upon the basis of real occult knowledge, the result of a partial initiation into the mysteries of the East. This is the character of Margrave in " A Strange Story," by Bulwer Lytton. It appears that the author makes Margrave himself not aware of the evils which his " double" plotted and carried into execution. At any rate, we have the warning that, before one seeks to transfer his consciousness to higher and inner planes of being, he should first become " pure in heart," as it is only such that truly "see their god." For the farther one retreats within the unfathomable depths of his being, the stronger and more powerful for good or evil do the forces which he employs become; and this from, a selfish, personal point of view alone, saying nothing of the irremediable woe he may work through employing ignorantly such a potent factor as the human will becomes in hypnotism.

From all the foregoing it will be apparent how completely the facts of hypnotism sustain the hypothesis that the human soul is an unit center of consciousness, using many vehicles. Of these the physical sense organs are only required to enable it to come into conscious relations with molecular planes of being. It also brings out, with startling distinctness, the fact that these sense organs limit the soul's conscious area, instead of widening it, thus completely negativing the materialistic hypothesis of the conscious functions of the soul being the result of molecular or chemical activities in the body. Equally important is the light it throws upon the composite nature of man, and the relation sustained to his center of consciousness by the various "souls'" vehicles or Principles through which that center may manifest. But, of course, the crowning usefulness of a study of hypnotic consciousness is that in demonstrating the independence of the human soul of its physical organs, it establishes as a necessary corollary the fact of its Reincarnation.

CHAPTER XII.

OBJECTIONS TO REINCARNATION.

THE chief objection to reincarnation is that we do not remember our past lives, as we ought to do if our " I am I" is a permanent center of consciousness, and merely passes from body to body upon the death of these. This at first sight seems a valid objection, for memory is a necessary link in constituting true self-consciousness. One chief argument advanced in proof of the existence of a soul is that there is a central something which binds states of consciousness into a continuous and connected unity, and without which unifying center they would of necessity remain simply states of consciousness; those present having no memory of nor hold upon those past, nor anticipation of those in the future. Therefore, we ought to remember our past if that past has been really continuous, and the objection is fatal unless the loss of the memory of our various personalities is fully explained.

This explanation is found in the compound nature of man. We have seen that the Higher Ego is only incarnated in a human-animal body for the purpose of descending to this plane of molecular consciousness; that there are really three evolutionary processes going on simultaneously in man—a physical, an intellectual or manasic, and a spiritual or monadic. With this third process the divine Monad is alone concerned. The second, or intellectual evolution, is that of the Higher Ego. The third appertains to the Lower Quaternary. While in man these three distinct streams of evolution are inextricably interblended, because to a greater or lesser degree each process is a factor in both the others, still they are distinct enough without being separate to fully account for non-remembrance of the one upon the plane of the other. Memory has been variously divided and classfied by psychologists, which divisions do not require analysis here. The one essential in any act of memory is the recording of a conscious experience. This record will and must differ with each plane of consciousness. The manasic plane being that of true self-consciousness, it takes here the self-conscious form; upon the physical, it records itself in other changes, which are physical rather than mental. None the less, however, are these changes the records of memory because below the self-conscious plane. The physical form and psychic characteristics, which represent the infinite variations in the entities upon the material plane of the Universe, constitute the memory of the conscious experiences of each entity recorded in these physical modifications. In the physical body of man is thus recorded each conscious experience undergone since he occupied that mass of jelly-like substance which we have reason to suspect was his first body, although the great mass of these experiences have of necessity been below the self-conscious plane.

Here, then, lies the secret of our not remembering our past lives. They have been and are entirely too much upon the physical plane to find other record than in those physical and lower psychic modifications of form and passional characteristics which lie too far below it to have any record upon the plane of manasic or true self-consciousness. The most of our conscious experiences are almost purely animal and while they are temporarily

recorded as separate experiences upon the brain cells of
each body, this record is of necessity destroyed as a self-
conscious register at death, and is only preserved upon
the corresponding register of its own plane—that of evolutionary modification.   The record is destroyed as a self-
conscious register for the reason that the personality has
no true self-consciousness.   The feeling of " I am I" of
our ordinary conscious experiences is reflected there by
the Higher Ego, as was explained in the chapter dealing
with that portion of the subject, and passes away entirely
either at or briefly following death.   All those ambitions,
"successes," and even intellectual achievements, no matter
how colossal they appear, if only intellectual, and not spiritualized, fall within the fatal line of non-permanency.
The life of a Napoleon, or of a Bacon, represents only the
lower animal faculties—intensely intellectualized, to be
sure, but having no greater claim to the spiritual remembrance of the Higher Ego than the humblest events in
the life of a clodhopper.   One must live upon the plane
of the Higher Manas to have a truly self-conscious memory; otherwise, he can and ought to expect the oblitera-
tion of his personal memory after devachanic existence
ceases and his next reincarnation occurs.   And just in
proportion as one does live in his higher Principles will
each personality live in the memory of the Higher Ego;
and, also, in proportion to his ability to reach this divine
plane of truly continuous self-consciousness while in the
body will he remember his past lives.

Those conscious experiences which represent the bor-
derland, as it were, between the higher and lower Manas,
or between the Individuality and Personality, are carried
forward as devachanic memories; but, being semi-spirit-

ual only, they are lost as self-conscious experiences upon reincarnation. They have all the permanence to which their mixed nature entitles them in the illusory but very happy recalling of them while in this subjective state. For the chief happiness of this condition lies in the power of the soul to take an earth memory or desire and make it the text, so to speak, upon which a series of thought pictures are constructed and which carry the unrealized desire or interrupted happiness to its highest ideal termination. The whole of Devachan is thus largely composed of these dramatized realizations of desires arising out of conscious experiences while in the body. It is only necessary that they should rise above the plane of gross animality for them to become the objects of this devachanic dramatization and realization.

That man's conscious experiences upon earth are so largely recorded upon the physical plane and in these karmic modifications of physical heredity, is a most beneficient provision of nature. So full of mistakes, errors, sins, and crimes is the past of, perhaps, every one of us, that the actual memory of it all carried forward in detail to each new life would overwhelm the soul with despair at the very outset. Nor is it essential to the conviction of our having lived before that we should remember each incident in our past lives, or even that we have lived before at all. Who remembers the first two or three years of his infancy? The fact that we were the same individual during this period of forgotten existence that we are now, none of us doubt, yet we would be sorely put about if we were required to furnish proof of this from memory. And even after this portion, how much do we remember of our life history if we attempt to recall it day by day, in

all its trifling minutiæ? Of the three score years and ten
of human existence in the body, few can accurately recall
the events of as many days—nay, hardly of as many min-
utes. All, except prodigies of memory, have practically
forgotten nine hundred and ninety-nine of every thousand
incidents of all their past. And yet the fact does not disturb us at all. We know that we are the result of this
experience we have come through; that our identity is
the same with that of the infant, the school boy, the
youth, the over-confident young man, the earnest, wiser
one of middle life, the tranquil, saddened one of old age.
Through it all the use of memory, being so largely physical, has been to link results together rather than incidents; to enable us to benefit by the past rather than to
be able to remember each particular portion of it.

This is the surest memory—the knowledge that the
crystallized results of what we have experienced are fully
and completely expressed in what we are now. Are we
prone to anger, and find it difficult to control fits of passion? Here is the memory of many a deed of violence
done under the dominance of our lower nature long ago.
Do we turn with horror away from injustice or extortion?
Be assured we are remembering the time when we ourselves were the sufferers from similar unjust acts. And
so on, through all the most delicate intricacies of our being. We are the creation of our past; and the nature we
have evolved is its memory. If we have gathered wisdom from the experiences of our lives, it is enough; in
just what the experience consisted is of little moment.
We may feel sure that under the guidance of the divine
law of Karma no experience has touched or ever can
touch us which we have not deserved in some capacity,

either in our individual, our family, our racial, or our national relations with our fellow-men.

Even before death, if we live to be old, nature anticipates the process by which she prepares us for new experiences, and we become again as little children. Our life work is done. All the knowledge which we can assimilate in this incarnation has been acquired, and so we return to the devachanic condition of childhood; and the mystery of involution, or the assimilating of the net results of experience, begins because the time for it has come and death has temporarily passed us by.

Another objection made from a purely emotional standpoint is that reincarnation separates us forever from those we have loved in this life. Nothing could be farther from the truth than this, for exactly the opposite occurs. Reincarnation, in common with every other phenomenon in nature, proceeds under the law of karma, or cause and effect, and we ourselves set up the causes whose effects are our rebirth not only in regard to time, but also as to those with whom we will find ourselves associated. These causes are largely, if not wholly, mental, and originate in the acts, emotions, and thoughts of our daily life. They, therefore, relate us karmically to those with whom we are thus daily associated, who are the subjects or objects of such thoughts or acts, and in exact proportion to the intensity of our feeling toward each of these, be that feeling either of love or of hatred. We can not set up causes which will bind our future life to those whom we have never met, nor have even known of mentally. This would be an absurd view to take of the law. We are, therefore, bound to those—and to those only—with whom we are most closely associated in either the bonds of love or hatred, for attraction and repulsion are but opposite poles or modes of motion of the same impersonal force, and are of equal strength. Therefore, the impersonal law of cause and effect will bring together those bound by bonds of hatred as surely as it will those related by ties of affection. This fact fully explains the otherwise inexplicable appearance of a single black sheep in an otherwise unblemished family, or those so-called "unnatural" hatreds between children and parents, or those which appear in any of the closely related ties of consanguinity.

The attraction thus set up between individuals by their associations and mental attitudes towards each other is as potent—and as patent—as that which binds atoms into the stable elements, so far beneath the mental plane. It is but another illustration of the unity of law upon all the planes of the Cosmos. So powerful is it that it can both draw souls to or from material existence, else its results would of necessity fail in uniting those karmically bound. We see its action in taking souls from the earth in those common cases where either the wife or husband quickly follows the other to the grave without apparent physiological reason. But more notable, because more opposed to the normal course of nature, are the numerous instances where a mother's death has been followed by so plain a loosening of its hold upon life by her young babe that even ignorant observers have recognized the fact that she was "drawing" it after her.

Of course, such cases are exceptions because out of the usual course of nature; but they are just those exceptions which prove the rule. For in the normal instances those associated would be likely to have subjective or devachanic lives of about the same duration. Therefore, if

in a group of karmically associated souls one were drawn
by karma and the closing of its subjective cycle to reincarnate, the center of attractive force thus transferred to
the material plane would be amply powerful to draw to it
others whose devachanic cycles were also closing; and the
close union, as in marriage, of certain of these might
easily set up a center of attraction sufficiently powerful to
bring to a close the Devachan of any Ego whose karma
demanded its association with such Egos thus incarnated.
Were this not the case a Devachan extending over 1,500
years would eternally separate, as far as material associations are concerned, an Ego from one whose spiritual nature entitled it to but 1,200 years in the same state, however close the ties of affection might have been during
life on earth.

As the length of life upon the earth is very greatly
modified by association with others, so is Devachan subject to similar modifications.   Racial or national karma
may subject us to a death by war, pestilence, or famine
which would not have been necessitated by our purely
personal karma, and the sanitary conditions of communi-
ties, even, shorten or lengthen the lives of the units
grouped in such karmic relations.   Especially is this so in
large cities.   San Francisco, for instance, has a certain
percentage of deaths due entirely to corrupt governments
having permitted peculation and dishonest work in its
sewer system.   Scores of lives are cut short yearly as a
direct karmic result of this community karma.   On the
other hand, scores and hundreds of lives are lengthened
by wise sanitary measures—especially in times of pestilence or epidemics.

If life be thus subject to modification on the material

plane, it is also subject to the same in Devachan, under the axiom that the action of any law must be universal. It is at least plain that there is nothing in the nature of Devachan to preclude the after association of individuals upon earth; but, on the contrary, that such associations are certain to continue so long as there is any attraction or repulsion between incarnated souls.

This is an infinitely wiser provision—attraction and repulsion—for human happiness than any merely physical ties of consanguinity. It ensures association so long as we desire it; it cuts us loose when we have become indifferent to any personality—thus grouping souls by their higher natures rather than upon a physical basis. Were the physical ties paramount, each child would demand an eternal association with its parents, they in turn with theirs, and so on back to some antediluvian ancestor, for whom the whole vast throng, except his immediate progeny, would feel the most profound indifference, as they also would for each other, except in a similar exceedingly limited relation. But soul attraction brings to each Ego its own; and as each parent, for instance, returns to incarnation attracting to it those children it really loved, these in turn, after paying their karmic debt, will attract their beloved, and so the links of human affection will remain forever unbroken until indifference or development in some new direction severs all old attractions.

A further objection to reincarnation, sometimes urged, is that it is unjust for us to suffer in this life the consequences of acts done in past ones which we have forgotten. To answer this it is only necessary to point out the absurdity of supposing that the mere forgetting of any act or crime absolves one from its consequences. Under this strange ethical view, it would be only necessary for a murderer to forget the crime he had committed to be relieved from all moral and legal responsibility. Could he not succeed in this himself it would only require that a hypnotizer should interpose, and the criminal thus made unconscious of his crime could be dragged off the very gallows itself. The law of cause and effect is impersonal, and, as far as we can conceive of consciousness, acts unconsciously. Often physical diseases are the result of causes set in action during the unconsciousness of sleep, yet the law inflicts the full penalty nevertheless. But the objection does not really deserve the recognition of an answer.

All possible objections to reincarnation must likewise disappear under the light of philosophy and logic, and it is only necessary that such objections be thus examined for the proof that this is an universal factor in nature and the method by means of which evolution proceeds to dawn upon the mind as clearly and convincingly as though one had set himself deliberately to prove its truth; for evolution and reincarnation are but aspects of the one eternal process in nature—infinite change.

CHAPTER XIII.

KARMA.

KARMA is the law of cause and effect, acting upon all planes. It is entirely impersonal in this action; and yet it acts wisely, intelligently and equitably, although the source of this intelligence and wisdom proceeds from the Unknowable. It does not reason, as we understand reasoning, nor is its wisdom accompanied by any mentality conceivable to human minds. Given a cause, and its corresponding effect will follow inevitably. Could this law be violated in but one instance, however trifling, the whole universe would fall into chaos, like a child's castle of cards.

Descartes founded his famous system of philosophy upon the postulate, *Cogito, ergo sum*. How much firmer a basis is afforded for the most profound conceptions of the universe in this law of Karma, that Effect follows Cause. It is a unit of measurement applicable to every conceivable point of space, every atom, every plane of being, every manifestation of consciousness in all this illimitable Cosmos. Taking its source in the Unknowable, yet having its action plainly perceivable upon our planes of life, it is the link which binds the knowable to the Unknowable. It is the one supreme testimony of unity and design, of intelligence and justice, in nature. Karma is but another name for the great Unknowable, CAUSELESS CAUSE.

Effect follows cause in the emergence of Cosmos from chaos; in the struggle for existence among the newly formed bodies of a solar system; in the "process of the suns" as they wing their way around their inconceivably vast orbits; in the aberrations of an Uranus, revealing the presence of a Neptune; in the involution and evolution of humanities; in the birth, life, and death of a man, of a molecule, or of a planetary system; in the racial, national, or social environments of the individual; in the presence of evil and injustice in the world; in the intellectual capacity of men; in their appetites, passions, and desires; in their spiritual aspirations; in their diseases and vices;— in short, in every conceivable juxtaposition or combination of thought, act or event, the Law is absolute; Karma, all-pervading. As far as the most daring generalizations of the human mind can reach, its sway is absolute. No exception can be postulated. Even the CAUSELESS CAUSE, the final goal of all rational philosophies, seems to yield obeisance to this law which proceeds out of its own abysses, for the manifestation of universes would appear to be only links in an Infinite Cycle of Necessity.

Once the universality of the action of Karma is recognized, we have a safe basis for our future explorations. It is an unfailing touchstone, wherewith we can test the truth of any proposition, whether religious, scientific, or philosophical. Its application to the problems of human life—to which, indeed, the term is commonly limited— constitutes the motive of this chapter. The importance of this phase of its study cannot be overestimated when we recognize that our whole life is but a succession of Nidanas, a chain of causes and effects, of which each effect becomes a cause in its own turn, and so on, in endless progression. No act, however trivial; no thought, however faint; no emotion, however fleeting—but is a cause, a bit of woof woven in the warp of our being, and giving it color and texture. An idle word—how often it changes a whole life; a thoughtless act, whose effects, or karma, follow us to and even beyond the grave! For it is a portion of this law that while any act or thought of ours may have its effect either within us, or externally upon others, the reaction, which is this effect become a cause again, must expend itself upon us individually. And it is most difficult to judge of the comparative magnitude of the causes we set in motion. A pebble thrown into the ocean seems a trifling cause, yet every separate drop in all the vast expanse of waters has to readjust its relations, as a direct and purely physical effect. And in addition to this permanent readjustment, the law of reaction, or restored equilibrium, requires every iota of force thrown off by the falling pebble to be returned to its source. In other words, the pebble has to receive a shock equal to that which it set in motion. In this simile, the original cause would be the falling pebble; its effect, the readjustment of the waters of the entire ocean; the reaction, or its personal Karma, the impulse of returning pressure, which, in relation to it, has become a cause again. In like manner, every act or thought of a man affects as a cause all other men in some degree, and this effect upon them will be returned to him, as a new cause, modifying his being to the extent of the effects it originally produced. .

It will thus be seen how impossible it is for any one to separate his Karma from that of his fellow-men. The interweaving and correlations are necessarily infinite; and naught but infinite wisdom, as embodied in the divine law of Karma, could mete out exact justice to us for all the multiform deeds of a lifetime. Isolation is a chimera. A Crusoe, on a desert island, will reach out to and affect the whole mass of humanity; for the pictures of his acts and thoughts, reflected in the astral light, will be re-reflected upon the physical plane, and influence to some degree the thought of the world. No man can think a good thought without the whole of humanity being somewhat the better for it; no man can sin against his higher nature without lowering the moral standard of the whole world to some extent.

This inevitable and necessary interblending of all our Karmas forms a true and scientific basis for the Theosophic conception of universal brotherhood; a reason, logical and necessary, for the practice of altruism. It also affords an occasion for the separation of karmic adjustments into classes, according as these relate to the individual himself or to his immediate or remote environments. Thus that aspect which views the Karma of all the units as one great whole would be termed world Karma; that which relates one to his race, his nation, his community, and his family, would be respectively, race, national, social, and family Karma; while the comparatively minute portion remaining would constitute his own, or his individual Karma. Yet this almost infinitesimal portion, this drop in the sea, is that with which we principally concern ourselves, as the very apotheosis of selfishness. Our hopes, our purification, our progress, seem, to our blinded eyes, of paramount importance; so subtle do vanity and self-esteem become when transmuted to higher planes. Bereft of intelligence, and depending upon brute force alone, of how much avail would be the strength of one man against the united sinews of his race, his nation,

or even against his community? In exact proportion is
the ratio of his Karma to that of his community, his nation, or his race. It is lost in the great whole; it is of
account only before that tribunal which "numbers the
hairs upon our heads." Let him who would attain personal "salvation," who would separate his Karma from
that of a wicked, sinful race by retiring to the jungle, or
within the recesses of his own selfish heart, and there
practicing the most austere virtues, go out and push
against the side of a mountain, in the hope of retarding
the revolution of the earth from West to East, for the one
effort will be of as much avail as the other.

Are there not thousands of men, whose personal
Karma would entitle them to be born under conditions as
delightful and just as any ever depicted by a Bellamy,
whose moral natures quiver under the outrageous ethics
of our social system every hour of their lives, yet who are
compelled by the national Karma which overwhelms them
to do the very acts they loathe; to live by taking the very
interest, profit, or rent which they abhor? Are there not
tens of thousands, whose sincere efforts in other lives to
attain to truth would have entitled them as units to its
revelation, who are nevertheless born in Christian or
pagan lands where the racial Karma offers only crude
dogmas or childish creeds? But has the justice of Karma
failed, then, because of this seeming injustice? Not so;
the efforts of these, even in the direction of truth and
purity, have been selfish; they have striven egotistically,
not altruistically; have worked for their personal salvation, not to save others. They have created good personal Karma, and Karma repays them to the uttermost
farthing, but they have done nothing to lighten the race

or national Karma, and they are engulfed in its floods. It was no chance thought, no accidental insertion of a "glittering generality," which declared the first object of the Theosophic Society to be the formation of a nucleus for an Universal Brotherhood. It evidences a wisdom and knowledge of the working of the law of Karma far transcending our petty conceptions. Altruistic effort is the law of spiritual progress because of the commingling of our Karmas; and even in selfish self-preservation, if from no higher motive, we ought to practice it. We recognize the injustice, the falsity, the hollowness of the social, ethical and religious customs of our time, yet we accept them and raise no protesting voice, because the whole world is against us, or we fancy it is. Can we charge it 'to the injustice of this divine law, then, if our next incarnation find us the son of a money-changer, with the lust of gold tainting our very mothers' milk? If the world is too hard for us now, will it not be so then? Let us exercise a little common sense in our study of Karma; let us remember that it is simply "cause and effect," and cannot but be just.

There is too much of the Christian idea of the entire separation of earthly from heavenly concerns abroad in the land. If we find this world in a bad state morally and ethically, we must logically expect to find it in a similar one when we reincarnate, especially if we did nothing towards lightening the world Karma. Cause precedes effect, on all planes. Our first duty, to be sure, is to make ourselves personally pure, because this is always at hand, and always practicable; our next, to strive for the elevation of our community, then our state, our nation, our race; each member of which ascending series includes

all below it, so that in working for humanity we are puri-
fying our race, our nation, our community, and ourselves.
And the effect of the causes we set up, of the Karma we
generate, is the greater as we ascend the series in motive.
It is this which gives the thought and the act force.
Thought is creative, and that which aims at the elevation
of the race will prove incomparably more potent a factor
for good than that directed towards petty or selfish aims.

We are but as drops in the great ocean of life. Our
very souls are tainted by the saltness and bitterness of
the floods about us. The bitterness of the whole ocean
can only be removed, and its waters made pleasant and
sweet, by the sweetening and purification of each separate
drop. No one can do this for another, and yet each can
only purify himself by unselfish work for others. How
beautifully grand is the LAW! What a magnificent stride
above and beyond the brute kingdom, where the
Buchners, Tyndalls, Darwins, and Huxleys would perforce
relegate us! The law of the animal kingdom is egotism;
the survival of the fittest; the cruel struggle for existence.
The law of Karma on the human plane is altruism and
selflessness, and we must recognize it or perish. For
cause and effect are at work in higher states of matter,
employing subtle and unperceived forces. The childhood
of our race has passed. We are fast reaching our majority, where we must take control of our own destinies, for
weal or woe. No longer the created, borne helplessly yet
safely along the mighty stream of evolution, we have become creators, and are karmically responsible for that
which we create. Our mouths have learned to voice the
WORD. Every thought and act is potent for good or evil;
the finer, "unscientific" forces of nature yield obedience

and obeisance whether we are aware of it or not. It is not enough that we recognize the universal presence of cause and effect, the omnipotence and omniscience of Karma; we must realize that we are free to change and direct this divine law, to our preservation or our destruction. This is a most important aspect of Karma, which must not be lost sight of. As the whole Cosmos is the thought of the Absolute, reflected in matter, so we, as a part and portion of that Absolute, exercise and employ creative potencies every hour of our lives. Shall we continue to do this ignorantly and aimlessly, or shall we take a firm hold upon our destinies and guide our souls into the haven of immortality? Certain it is that we must make the decision soon, for we are pilgrims in the cycle of necessity; we must go forward either to safety or destruction. And this is not predicated upon the emotionalism of some wailing Jeremiah of ancient, or Buchanan of modern, times; but simply and entirely for the reason that EFFECT follows CAUSE. One is the upper, the other the nether mill-stone of fate, and we are inextricably caught between them.

It will be at once evident that, holding as it does to the absolute sway of cause and effect upon every plane of the universe, physical, mental and spiritual, Theosophy stands in irreconcilable antagonism to the Christian dogma of vicarious atonement. And herein is the chief reason why most Theosophists refuse to ally themselves, even under the name of Christian Theosophists, with the churches of to-day. They recognize fully that Christianity is an humane and altruistic effort to improve the condition of mankind morally and spiritually; but this error of the divinity of Christ and his vicarious atonement is too basic in its nature, too far-reaching in its karmic results, to be passed over in a silence which might be construed into acquiescence.   Each time that a repentant sinner is assured that the effects of causes he himself set in operation can be nullified by forgiveness from any source, he is being taught an untruth which can not but imperil the future development of his soul.   Each time a priest pronounces absolution over some terrified wretch whom the shadow of the gallows, perhaps, has frightened into " repentance" after a long life of selfishness and crime, he assumes an authority and a power which is absolutely at variance with the law to which he owes his own existence. The marked contrast between the philosophical doctrine of Karma and the dogma of vicarious atonement has been well set forth by a recent writer.*   He says:

"There is a wide gulf between the Buddhist doctrine of Karma and the Christian teaching regarding the dispensing of reward and punishment.   In proportion to that difference the moral control exercised on human actions must differ in a corresponding degree. Karma, according to Buddhism and other Eastern schools of philosophy, is an inviolable, natural law, which controls the lives of all sentient beings in the Universe, and which in its turn is not governed by any superior force or being.   As long as thoughts and actions last so long will their results, or Karma, prevail.   The least thing moved in space has a certain effect on the particles floating thereon; the slightest motion in water gives rise to ripple after ripple until the force thereof is expended; the gentlest sound sends forth vibrations producing change somewhere;   and the very smallest thought has also its tendency to disturb either the thinker or the object thought of.   The further such research is extended, the more will the application of the karmic law to human actions prove to be as true and natural as are the laws of attraction and gravitation.

*The Buddhist.

Then, when it is known by man that all his thoughts and actions have certain tangible and perceptible effects, and that these effects have a rebounding tendency, or that they remain registered in his *manas skandha*, to cleave to him in whatever condition he may be hereafter, a lasting and powerful impression of awe and veneration must be the natural result created in his mind. He who is morally convinced of the inevitable effect and danger of certain thoughts and actions, and of the reward which awaits him through certain others, must be more deeply impressed in mind than another who entertains no such belief. The Christian doctrine of the absolution of sins is a total cancellation of the past—whether there be crimes of the blackest type or not—by an act of momentary repentance, which places the wretched moral leper on a par with the most exalted saint. It is apparent from this fact that the votaries of Christianity must rely more upon supernatural magic to ease themselves of a life burden of ugly sins than upon an uncheckered course of pure, moral life. If this extraordinary feat could be scientifically or otherwise demonstrated, there are many in these glowing Eastern climes who would readily embrace Christianity."

The writer also shrewdly draws attention to the fact, emphasized in the first portion of this chapter in regard to the separation by Christians of earthly from heavenly concerns, that we do not apply the doctrine of the remission of sins in our treatment of criminals to any very demoralizing extent, and that the effect of such an application of the laws of heaven to earthly conditions would be to immeasurably increase lawlessness and crime.

The law of Karma, too, being impersonal in its action, solves two of the greatest puzzles over which Christianity has pondered in vain. These are the presence of evil in a world created by an all-wise and all-powerful Creator, and free will consistent with omniscient fore-knowledge. No Christian theology has ever satisfactorily explained

why an omnipotent God did not devise some means
whereby he might save from the eternal flames lost souls
which his omniscient knowledge informed him would
eventually be eternally lost.   And if God, from all
eternity, knew a thing would happen, then it had to
happen; and just how this could be reconciled with human
free will was another of those conundrums whose distinguishing peculiarity is that they have no answer.

The Presbyterian branch, of all the protesting churches,
recognizes the logical necessity which follows postulating
both omnipotence and omniscience of a personal deity,
and boldly avows its belief in predestination, or fatalism.
As quoted from J. H. Connelly, in the *Key to Theosophy*,
their Confession of Faith declares:

"By the decree of God and for the manifestation of his glory, some
men and angels are predestinated unto everlasting life, and others
foreordained to everlasting death.

"These angels and men thus predestinated and foreordained are particularly and unchangeably designed; and their number is so certain
and definite that it cannot be either increased or diminished......As
God hath appointed the elect to glory, neither are any other re-
deemed by Christ, effectually called, justified, adopted, and sanctified
and saved, but the Elect only.

"'The rest of mankind God was pleased, according to the unsearch-
able counsel of his own will, whereby he extendeth or withholdeth
mercy as he pleaseth, for the glory of his sovereign power over his
creatures, to pass by and to ordain them to dishonor and wrath for
their sin to the praise of his glorious justice !'"

This is not the ravings of some hypochondriacal, half-
insane prophet; it is a part of the PRESBYTERIAN CONFES-
SION OF FAITH, and is accepted to-day by a very large
class of intelligent, educated, and refined gentlemen and
loving, lovable women, who would no more do that which

they declare their God does, daily and hourly, than they would transform themselves into fiends. It is the inevitable and logical outcome of a belief whose very foundations are laid in error.

Is Presbyterianism alone in its attributing injustice to God which it would deem barbarous and unfeeling in man? By no means. No human bar of justice, imperfect as is the attribute in our breasts in its present stage of development, would ever doom any one to the pangs of ETERNAL perdition and suffering for any act, however dreadful or cruel. But all Christian sects, without exception, send comparatively innocent souls to this eternal damnation for simply being unable to believe in and accept this awful Jehovah whom they have set up for worship. In his profession as a physician, the writer has, time and again, known little infants, which some unforeseen accident deprived of life before receiving baptism, refused burial in "sanctified" ground by the great Catholic Church and condemned to the woes of eternal torment on account of this omission—a little water sprinkled on an unconscious infant deciding its eternal destiny! What a conception of the philosophy of existence the believers in such dogmas must have! African fetich worship is more reasonable. But how can any system of faith or philosophy arrive at reasonable or logical conclusions whose very base is founded in untruth and error? Like a mariner whose compass is untrue, and who, therefore, only deviates the more the farther he sails, so Christian creeds, being founded in error, can only hope to increase their separation from truth the farther they pursue any train of explanation or reasoning.

Let it be understood, once for all, that by Christianity,

throughout this chapter, the writer refers to the modern creeds parading under this falsely assumed title. The teachings of the Essenes, of whom Christ was one, are eminently Theosophic in many particulars, and both Christ and Paul taught, as we have undoubted reason for believing, pure Theosophy to an inner circle of disciples. Only to the multitude " spake he in parables." Christ was continually referring to the god within him, his " Father," which, by implication at least, he taught his disciples that they also possessed, for " the things that I do shall ye do also, and greater because I go to my Father." But he nowhere refers to himself as the Creator of heaven and earth, as the purely personal egotism of his latter-day followers has led them to assume.

There is no place, then, in Theosophy for the vicarious atonement, or the setting aside the law of cause and effect, which is the very soul of the Christian creeds of to-day. Justice is not mocked by an impossible and unphilosophical "forgiveness" whose sole essential is repentance. As well might a dyke repent that it had burst and let in the sea. Repentance itself too often consists of a feeling of fear of the consequence of our act, rather than a real regret for what we have done. As J. H. Connelly further remarks:

"The sinner is told that he must also repent, but nothing is easier than that. It is an amiable weakness of human nature that we are quite prone to regret the evil we have done when our attention is called, and we have either suffered from it ourselves or enjoyed its fruits. Possibly, close analysis of the feeling would show us that which we regret is rather the necessity which seemed to require the evil as a means of attainment of our selfish ends than the evil itself.

"Attractive as this prospect of casting our sins at the foot of the Cross may be to the ordinary mind, it does not commend itself to the theosophic student. He does not apprehend why the student by attaining knowledge of his evil can thereby merit any pardon for or the blotting out of his past wickedness; or why repentance and future right living entitle him to a suspension in his favor of the universal law of relation between cause and effect. The results of his evil deeds continue to exist; the suffering caused to others by his wickedness is not blotted out. The Theosophical student takes the result of wickednes upon the innocent into his problem. He considers not only the guilty person, but his victims.

"Karma, also, rewards merit as unerringly as it punishes demerit. It is the outcome of every act, thought, word and deed, and by it men mold themselves, their lives and happenings. Eastern philosophy rejects the idea of a newly-created soul for every baby born. It believes in a limited number of monads, evolving and growing more and more perfect through their assimilation of many successive personalities. These personalities are the product of Karma, and it is by Karma and reincarnation that the human monad in time returns to its source—absolute Deity."

Karma is inextricably interwoven with reincarnation. Without the latter, it would be impossible to assume, at least in human affairs, that cause is invariably followed by effect. The many murderers who escape detection, the hordes of those who grow rich through robbing the poor, the whole tendency of an age where honesty is not the best policy, if one would win in the mad race for wealth, all show but too plainly that one life is too short for exact justice to be meted out to any one. But, "though the mills of the gods grind slowly, yet they grind exceedingly small," and there is no more beautiful or more hope-inspiring aspect of Karma than this which shows it capable of biding its time. Its eternal patience must seem awful to him who is waiting his turn at the mill. There is no escape. A wheat kernel has been known to lie thousands

of years in the wrappings of a mummy, and then germ-
inate upon being restored to warmth and moisture.   This
is the key to and the proof of that which we term delayed
Karma.   Desire is the most potent of all forces, and we
may be assured that the attractions for evil things generated by the usurer or murderer will prove causes which
will find the conditions for becoming effects in some
future birth.   So the evils which we uncomplainingly
suffer now will be recompensed to the utmost in some
bright and beautiful, though it may be far-off, life.   What
is time to the heir of eternity?   Thus the everlasting
patience of Karma assures us that no effort we make can
be without its ultimate reward; that no wrong we inflict
can escape final punishment.

In closing this brief chapter upon a subject that vol-
umes would leave unexhausted, we can do no better than
to quote from the Teacher to whom the Western world is
indebted for this revival of an almost forgotten truth.   In
the Secret Doctrine, Madame Blavatsky writes:

"Yes; 'our destiny is written in the stars!'   Only the closer the
union between the mortal reflection, MAN, and his celestial PROTO-
TYPE, the less dangerous the external conditions and subsequent
reincarnations—which neither Buddhas nor Christs can escape.   This
is not superstition, least of all is it fatalism.   The latter implies a
blind course of some still blinder power, and man is a free agent
during his stay on earth.......Those who believe in Karma
have to believe in destiny, which, from birth to death, every man is
weaving, thread by thread, around himself, as a spider does his cob-
web; and this destiny is guided either by the heavenly voice of the
invisible prototype outside of us, or by our more intimate astral or
inner man, who is but too often the evil genius of the embodied
entity called man.   Both these lead on the outward man, but one of
them must prevail; and from the very beginning of the invisible

affray, the stern and implacable law of compensation steps in and takes its course, faithfully following the fluctuations. When the last strand is woven and man is seemingly enwrapped in the network of his own doing, then he finds himself completely under the empire of this self-made destiny......There is no return from the paths Karma cycles over; yet these paths are of our own making, for it is we, collectively or individually, who prepare them. Karma-Nemesis is the synonym of PROVIDENCE, minus design, goodness and every other *finite* attribute or qualification, so unphilosophically attributed to the latter. An Occultist or a philosopher will not speak of the goodness nor cruelty of providence, but, identifying it with Karma-Nemesis, he will teach that nevertheless it guards the good and watches'over them in this, as in future lives; and that it punishes the evil doer—aye, even to his seventh re-birth. So long, in short, as the effect of his having thrown into perturbation even the smallest atom in the infinite world of harmony, has not been finally readjusted. For the only decree of Karma—an eternal and immutable decree—is absolute harmony in the world of matter as it is in the world of spirit. It is not, therefore, Karma which rewards or punishes, but it is we who reward and punish ourselves according to whether we work with, through, and along with nature, abiding by the laws on which that harmony depends, or—break them.

"Nor would the ways of Karma be inscrutable were men to work in union and harmony instead of disunion and strife. For our ignorance of these ways—which one portion of mankind calls the ways of Providence, dark and intricate, while another sees in them the action of blind fatalism, and a third, simple chance, with neither gods nor devils to guide them—would surely disappear, if we would but attribute all these to their correct cause......With right knowledge......two-thirds of the world's evil would vanish into thin air. Were no man to hurt his brother, Karma-Nemesis would have neither cause to work, nor weapons to act through. It is the constant presence in our midst of every element of strife and opposition, and the division of races, nations, tribes, societies and individuals into Cains and Abels, wolves and lambs, that is the chief cause of

the ways of Providence. We cut these numerous windings in our
destinies daily with our own hands, while we imagine that we are
pursuing a track on the royal high road of respectability and duty,
and then complain of these ways being so intricate and dark. We
stand bewildered before the mystery of our own making, and the
riddles of life that we *will not* solve, and then we accuse the great
Sphynx of devouring us. But, verily, there is not an accident of our
lives, nor a mishappen day, nor a misfortune that could not be
traced back to our own doings in this or another life.

"The law of Karma is inextricably interwoven with that of Reincarnation...... It is only this doctrine that can explain the mysterious problem of good and evil, and reconcile man to the terrible and
apparent injustice of life. Nothing but such certainty can quiet our
revolted sense of justice. For, when one acquainted with the noble
doctrine looks around him and observes the inequalities of birth and
fortune, of intellect and capacities ; when one sees honor paid to
fools and profligates, on whom fortune has heaped her favors by
mere privilege of birth, and their nearest neighbor, with all his
intellect and noble virtues—far more deserving in every way—perishing for want and for lack of sympathy ;—when one sees all this and
has to turn away, helpless to relieve the undeserved suffering, one's
ears ringing and one's heart aching with the cries of pain around
him, that blessed knowledge of Karma alone prevents him from
cursing life and men as well as their supposed Creator. This law,
whether conscious or unconscious, predestines nothing and no one.
It exists from and in eternity truly, for it is eternity itself; and as
such, since no act can be co-equal with eternity, it cannot be said to
act, for it is action itself. It is not the wave which drowns the man,
but the personal action of the wretch who goes deliberately and
places himself under the impersonal action of the laws that govern
the ocean's motion. Karma creates nothing, nor does it design. It
is man who plants and creates causes, and karmic law adjusts the
effects, which adjustment is not an act but universal harmony tend-
ing ever to resume its original position, like a bough which, bent
down too forcibly, rebounds with corresponding vigor. If it happen

to dislocáte the arm that tried to bend it out of its natural position, shall we say it is the bough which broke our arm, or that our own folly has brought us to·grief? Karma has never sought to destroy intellectual and individual liberty, like the god invented by the monotheists. It has not involved its decrees in darkness purposely to perplex man, nor shall it punish him who dares to scrutinize its mysteries. On the contrary, he who unveils, through study and meditation, its intricate paths, and throws light on those dark ways, in the windings of which so many men perish owing to their ignorance of the labyrinth of life, is working for the good of his fellowmen. Karma is an absolute and eternal law in the world of manifestation; and as there can only be one absolute, one eternal, ever-present cause, believers in Karma cannot be regarded as atheists or materialists, still less as fatalists, for Karma is one with the Unknowable, of which it is an aspect, in its effects in the phenomenal world."

The confusion of Karma with predestination or fatalism can easily be avoided by remembering that our Karma is predestined to the extent that we must experience the effects of causes we have set up in past lives, only. Yet, even while suffering, this effect changes into a new cause, according to our mental attitude towards it. Thus he who has been sent by deeds done in past lives into a diseased body, by his fortitude in bearing this just effect of his own acts can rise on the "stepping-stones of his dead self to higher things"; while, by rebellion and railings against what he is pleased—or taught—to call "fate," he enacts new causes whose effects can but be unfavorable.

CHAPTER XIV.

ETHICAL CONCLUSIONS.

THE truth of the reincarnation of the human soul carries with it as necessary corollaries most important ethical conclusions. It establishes a philosophic and legitimately scientific basis for human conduct—something that the world has not had since the perversion of the teachings of Christ, during the second and third centuries of this era. Even at that time the real gnosis underlying Christ's tenets was only trusted in the hands of an inner circle of disciples, and by no means given to the world at large. "Cast not your pearls before swine," taught this Master, which reservation may have afforded the very opportunity for perversion by prohibiting the giving out of the real truth when erroneous teachings began to creep in through the ignorance of the Church Fathers. Certainly, not within the records of modern history has there been such an unveiling of Isis, such light thrown upon the problems of human life, as in the writings of Madame H. P. Blavatsky, which goes to prove that human necessity must have been very urgent for the Custodians of the Archaic Wisdom to have permitted this profuse giving out of sacred and secret teachings.

At any rate, enough light has been thrown upon man's relation to his fellow-men and to nature to afford a sound basis for human ethics. As a part of the great Whole, as an emanation from a higher Logos, and constituting himself a lower one, a knowledge of these relations is of infinite importance in its determining influence upon not only his highest hopes, aspirations, ambitions, but also upon his every thought and act in his daily life. Knowing this life to be but a school for preparing him for a higher and happier one, and that this happier existence cannot be attained by any sycophantic adulation, cajoling of or forgiveness by an imaginary Jehovah, but must be won under the iron law of cause and effect; and, further, that, like pupils in our public schools, he will be kept in this grade of sin and suffering by continually reincarnating until he himself earns his promotion to a higher one— man cannot but begin to examine his motives more closely, to pay some attention to the debtor and creditor account of a karma as accurate as it is inevitable.

Under the short-sighted Western conception of but one existence upon this earth, the numerous and grossly palpable failures in justice, in human affairs, have exerted a most pernicious influence upon human ethics. Solomon, indeed, declared that he had never "seen the righteous forsaken, nor his seed begging bread"; but the very reverse obtains under our social system, in which, as caustically remarked by Madame Blavatsky, we have made of vice an art and of selfishness a basis for ethics. We loudly claim that "honesty is the best policy," while thousands of millionaires who have come dishonestly by every penny of their hoards not only go down to peaceful and honored graves, but with the assurance—signed, sealed, executed, and the "cash" equivalent receipted for—of eternal happiness in the future.

Under the broader view, all these apparent failures in justice are recognized as only apparent, and not real, human self-respect is restored; and the intuitive belief that honesty is the best policy, obscured by the one-life hori-

zon, becomes magnificently demonstrated as these horizons are seen to stretch away into an infinite perspective.
Recognizing that we ourselves have made the bitter present by an unwise past, that we have not been unjustly and
causelessly born into this sphere of existence the helpless
victims of fate or of accident, we can set ourselves cheerfully to right by the light of the broader conception,
environments, both physical and mental, which we know
to be but the meting out of exact and impersonal justice to
us. By the light of Reincarnation and Karma, we perceive that the social injustices with which our civilization
is now cursed are rooted too deeply to be plucked out by
merely changing our laws. Human desires and motives
must be radically changed, and this can only be done by
making man aware of his true nature and god-like destiny.
Then he will recognize that all the evils which now
threaten to engulf humanity in a sea of anarchy and
bloodshed arise wholly out of yielding to the dominance
of the animal portion of his being—are on the animal
plane—and that all appeals to force or violence can only
still further arouse and strengthen those brutal elements
to control and spiritualize, which is the chief reason for
incarnation upon this earth. Social and political reform
must proceed, like every other process in nature, from
within without; and when the inner desire to act justly
shall have arisen, the outer act will quickly conform.
Meanwhile, no effort to show the real unity and solidarity
of humanity is of as great importance as the popularizing
of the teachings of Reincarnation, which distinguishes the
true man and his necessities from the false one with his
illusionary ambitions, and Karma, which shows that social
as well as all other evolution takes place under the law of
cause and effect, and cannot but act justly.

Aside from social and political considerations, the twin truths of Reincarnation and Karma, when once clearly comprehended, satisfy the religious element which is, or ought to be, so deeply engrafted in every human heart. It has been well and truly said that " religion is for the wise, and superstition for the ignorant"; and within these teachings only is to be found that food which will supply the need of rational and philosophical men for a scientific and philosophical religion. Therefore, from the religious standpoint, this inquiry into the nature and functions of the soul is amply justified. Blind faith alone fails ; creeds are but idle patterings and empty sounds; man must know his destiny, or the incentive to upward exertion is largely paralyzed. Reason teaches us that death cannot transport us where we are not now; cannot act as a kind of moral filter, that in some miraculous way will remove the impurities of our lower nature, and fit us for habita- tion in some high or " heavenly " sphere, nor, failing this, transport us to some inconceivably horrible hell. The chain of life is formed of continuous links. We have become what we are by an infinite series of past lives; we have to work out our future destiny by an infinite ser- ies of lives to come. Here, where we are struggling in the bonds of matter, is our only " hell," the law of cause and effect our sole punisher, and " heaven " our release from sensuous existence either temporarily by death, or wholly through our evolving beyond sensuous necessities. The warning voice of conscience is but the voice of our Higher Ego, speaking as the result of actual experience and wisdom. And because the seat of conscience is, of necessity, in the Higher Ego, it therefore seems to us as though it came from some outside source, when it is in

reality our true self, vainly endeavoring to guide and control the coarse and unwieldly physical machine, to which
it finds itself karmically attached, and with which it is
therefore so closely inter-related that the one must ever
react upon the other. Out of this action and reaction
grows the real battle of life; the tide turning now this
way and now that. Knowing all this, man will rest
secure in the Divine law of cause and effect, which
neither punishes nor rewards, but wisely, justly, and inex-
orably adjusts each cause to its corresponding effect.
Knowing himself to be the arbiter of his own destiny, he
will cease to complain; cease to attribute his sorrows and
sufferings to the ways of a mysterious providence; and
recognizing that nothing has come nor can come to him
which is not his own by virtue of having created or caused
it, he will begin the warfare against his lower nature with
a strength of purpose and determination to succeed impossible before this realization. The worlds, the stars, and
suns will no longer be created solely for him, but rather
he for them. Even the strife in nature, the cruel struggle
for existence, will not seem so dreadful when he realizes
that nothing is really slain; that "he who slays and he
who thinks himself slain are alike deceived." Nor will he
longer trust to forms and creeds, but instead will retire to
the inner chamber of his own heart and worship silently
that which is equally at the basis of his soul as it is at the
base of the flower or stone, the Unknowable, Inconceivable Causeless Cause.

Realizing through these teachings the actual, dynamic
brotherhood of mankind; that the fall of one proportion-
ately hurts and retards the advancement of the race; and
that the attainment of the goal of assured immortality by

but one faithful, unselfish, sacrificing soul shortens in some degree the weary path to be trod by his brother men—he will merge all merely selfish longings in the realization of the help to others thus afforded by his own toil, and patiently and tranquilly work for Humanity, unterrified by life and undismayed by death.

Rightly comprehended, then, Reincarnation comes to us as a message of hope, of love, and of Divine encouragement. To those who so pitifully cling to youth and the pleasures of the young, it holds the promise of renewed youth, life after life. To him who has been conquered in the battle of life, it offers other opportunities for further and more efficient battling. To all it promises that no effort shall be lost, nor without its reward; that the aspirations unable to be realized now shall find full fruition then; that the very loved ones of this life, so rudely torn from us by death, will be again attracted by and drawn to us in our next earth-life, to renew the interrupted associations.

But the great, the all-important lesson Reincarnation teaches is that our powers are infinite, our opportunities eternal, and our goal god-like. Our progress is illimitable, and death but a brief rest in a way-side inn, as we journey along. After each death, upon reincarnating, we take up our earth life at the precise point we laid it aside; thus ever increasing our wisdom through continuous experience. A perfect knowledge of earth limitations requires, as we have seen, that each man should undergo every possible phase of human experience; should subdue every variety of human passion, and resist every form of temptation. Only by reincarnation is it possible to do this; to round out and develop patience, fortitude, pity, benevolence, and a host of other god-like attributes; all of which have to be refined out of the crucible of actual experience and suffering.   One life is all too short for the lessons of sympathy and love we have to learn, ere we develop compassion for the woes of others from the fires of our own purification, from the ashes of our sacrificed passions. One life is all too short for us even to approximate that condition of spirituality which would permit us to exist for a moment on planes where earthly concerns and desires are utterly unknown.   After the great deep had brought forth life in its waters, it took ages for the water-breathing vertebrates to so accustom themselves to the purer, rarer air that life in its thin gases became possible for them.   So with man's spiritual nature.   How absurd, how impossible, to fancy him as capable of living under spiritual conditions before he has developed the spiritual power!   He must conquer every earthly passion, subdue every mortal desire, and keenly realize the unsatisfying nature, the instability, of material life, before he can hope to attain to the life spiritual.   At present man is little more than a savage in his instincts, appetites, and passions.   Let him first become a MAN, with all the magnificent meaning and prophecy in the word, before he aspires to the Elysean fields of the Gods.   Yet these fields are surely his, both by birthright and as the meed of toil and suffering, if he but persist in the warfare, if he but prove faithfnl to the one talent placed in his keeping during this life; renewing his courage and hope in the knowledge that greater and still greater opportunities will be afforded him in future lives by the return of his soul to earth through the golden gate of REINCARNATION.

APPENDIX.

EMBRYOLOGY, AND REINCARNATION.

WHILE not falling strictly within the purpose of this work, there are certain facts connected with the very beginnings of physical life that are of sufficient interest and importance to merit brief notice. For these facts the world is indebted to scientific investigation; for the explanation of them, it must look to the philosophies of the East.

All life in the organic kingdoms of nature proceeds from a cell; this cell being in essence a unit body of protoplasm. Subjected to chemical analysis after death, Protoplasm differs in its chemical constituents in no wise from matter undoubtedly belonging to the so-called inorganic kingdom beneath, thus showing plainly that in matter itself is not to be found the cause of the subsequent evolution of form and function; but that something besides mere chemical properties has been added to the material molecules. This is further shown by the fact that the chief difference in the simple protozoic or protophytic cell and the highly organized and synthesized plant or animal consists in the fact that in the cell the function is complex, while in the plant or animal it is the form. The beginnings of life thus traced down to the unit cell of protoplasm seems a very simple and basic starting point, when, in fact, it is the form only which has become simplified, the function has been plunged into a more intricate maze of obscurity. That which in the higher organism was the work of hosts of differentiated cells and complex organs, is in the cell all accomplished without any such aid; the simple, unorganized, undifferentiated speck of Protoplasm performing many of the complex and all of the necessary functions of life without any of that specialization of labor, in the complex form. Desiring to change its locality, limbs are protruded for the occasion; feeling hungry, a temporary stomach is manufactured, and so on; all the varied functions of locomotion, nutrition, reproduction, digestion, with many others, being done by means of the same undifferentiated protoplasmic substance, showing clearly that there is an inner power merely using the protoplasm to exhibit these functions. It is thus seen that the function which seemed so simple when the form was complex has almost passed beyond the possibility of explanation when the form in turn has become simple.

It is evident that the idea of all subsequent evolution of form is potentially present in the first simple cell, and that all modification or differentiation which follows is but the slow expression of this ideal potency in form.   Therefore, an entity utterly without experience upon this plane would of necessity begin in the humblest forms, and only very gradually modify these as the result of widened conscious experience.   The fact that in the lowly forms of life the function greatly exceeds the form in complexity shows conclusively that there is an inner entity synthesizing these functions, and that evolution in all its phases is but the outer response to the inner idea, and, as ideas necessitate an ideator, an inner entity is therefore necessitated.

In these humblest beginnings of life, too, are to be found many analogies to and confirmations of the tenet of Theosophy that everything in the Universe proceeds out of Unity and will rebecome Unity when the Universe disappears objectively and enters upon its subjective cycle, or Pralaya.   In its first differentiation or manifestation this Unity evolved Duality, which Duality, together with the Force which brought it about, constitute the three Basic Aspects or Hypostases of the Absolute.   Transposing these terms to the physical plane, in Protoplasm may be recognized the analogue of Primordial Substance;   it being, in its relation to this plane, homogeneous and capable of differentiation into any organic form, no matter how complex the latter may be.   The intelligence which guides and the force which brings about further evolutionary processes are the correspondences to the Conscious-Aspect and Force-Aspect of the Causeless Cause, respectively.

Taking up some of the processes of Embryology, we can find therein the analogies to the Creative processes upon even the highest planes.   Thus the Basic Unity is shown in the unit cell of protoplasm; duality supervenes in its first and entirely inexplicable fission.   In its further differentiation into ectoderm endoderm and mesoderm, there is a purely physical correspondence of a law which obtains upon the plane of the very highest differentiation.   In the central development of Spencer, may be recognized the archaic symbol of the Point in the Circle; in the axial, the point has become a line or diameter, and so on.   The symbology of the East becomes luminous with meaning once it is intelligently applied to nature's processes.

Within and because of this Primordial Duality arise all of those polar opposites, such as attraction and repulsion, positive and negative states, spirit and matter, and—upon the purely physical plane

—male and female. That sex is a differentiation upon the physical plane only, is shown by the fact that all reproduction is at first purely asexual. Sex, upon this plane, corresponds to a principle which causes differentiation upon those higher. As the' Protoplasm responds more and more to the inner energy, there is first the cell specialization for the reproductive act, and then this differentiation, with many variants and partial reversions to the primal type, becomes extended to individuals. Sexual differentiation is but another instance of the widening of conscious area through experience of the "pairs of opposites." As a purely physical process, the theory of anabolic and katabolic differentiation of energy very probably explains its origin; but the inner cause of the anabolism and katabolism is still as much a mystery as ever unless we recognize the inner entity undergoing conscious experience in the only school and by the sole method of which we can conceive—that of experience of the "opposites," by virtue of which the very Universe itself exists. Sex exemplifies the positive and negative forces or aspects of the Absolute upon the purely physical plane.

That there is an inner entity thus continuously widening its conscious area through evolution is the only logical deduction from the phenomena of evolution itself. All of that careful examination and cautious ratiocination by which it is proven that the fowl, for instance, has been evolved from the fish, only emphasizes the fact that it must be the same inner entity which was the fish, and which is now the fowl. If it has been necessary to take the first steps towards constructing a bird by building a fish form, this proves that the idea of the bird was present, and slowly modifying the fish throughout its entire existence as a fish. To disconnect the fish from the bird for a single moment is to overthrow the entire evolutionary process. If the one is really the modification of the other, then both throughout their respective evolutionary cycles are as much the same entity as are the child and the man, or the butterfly and the caterpillar. Either they are connected causally by the evolutionary modification of the one from the other, or they are not. If, as evolution declares, they are thus connected, then it is the same entity which has, during the whole period, been slowly evolving different and more perfect forms. There is no logical escape from this conclusion.

Without pursuing further the subject of reproduction in general, there are many facts in human embryological detail which go to prove that this process is a specific obedience of the outer Protoplasm to an inner, intelligent force. Among these is the wonderful response of the uterus to the stimulation of the developing embryo. If this were a purely mechanical stimulation, due to the presence of the embryo, other foreign bodies ought to call out the same or a similar response. But this is not the case. The womb will quickly expel any invader of its cavity; even a tumor in its walls is often extruded as a polypus. Instead, however, of attempting to expel the fecundated cell, every effort is made by the uterus to retain and nourish it. There is poured out from the uterine walls an abundant supply of the most highly nutritious, albuminous pabulum from which the growing embryo builds its marvelously perfect body; each tissue under the guidance of the inner entity differentiating out of the common protoplasmic stock.

At this point, perhaps, it may be well to call attention to the grossly incorrect "scientific" teaching concerning the nutrition of the fetus, if but to show how carefully one must examine even the most unquestioned scientific statements if he would avoid steering into the Charybdis of dogmatic assertion in endeavoring to keep clear of the Scyllæ of ignorance. This teaching is to the effect that the fetus is nourished through the placenta. The true *modus operandi* was discovered by the author during a series of experiments extending over 1882-'83, and was first published in the *American Journal of Obstetrics* in 1884, in a paper entitled "A New Theory of Fetal Nutrition," from which I shall freely quote. This theory is, that once conception has taken place the fetus is nourished by absorbtion of nutritive material secreted and poured into the uterine cavity from its walls, and that the office of the placenta is purely respiratory, or an oxygen carrier and carbonic acid gas remover. The facts which prove this to be the correct view are:

1. The constant presence of nutritive substances in the amniotic fluid during the entire period of gestation. 2. The certainty of this fluid being absorbed by a developing fetus constantly bathed in it. 3. The permeability of the digestive tract at an early period, and the necessary entrance therein, according to the laws of hydrostatics, of the albuminous amniotic fluid. 4. The presence of meconium in the intestine, urine in the bladder, and bile in the upper intestine—all in their normal locations. 5. The mechanical difficulties opposing direct nutrition through the placenta. 6. The absence of a placenta until the third month, and its entire absence in the non-placental mammalia. 7. The maternal source of the fluid, as shown by the hydrorrhœas, etc., of pregnancy.

The presence of meconium—a residue after absorbtive digestion—and of urine and bile are all incompatible with the theory of nutritive material being conveyed to the embryo through the placenta; but the most prominent fact enumerated above is the constant presence of albumen in the amniotic fluid. This constant presence means that it is not accidental. One of the most plausible theories as to the uses of the amniotic fluid is that it constitutes a kind of water cushion to protect the embryo from mechanical injury. This is no doubt one use. But if this were all we would not find nature supplying a very precious and costly—to the mother—ingredient, or albumen. This would be worse than a blunder. It would be a crime against maternity. If we suppose, with Lusk and a host of other authors, that the source of this fluid "is at first simply an exudate from the tissues of the fetus," and, later, "urine secreted and voided by the fetus," we have the highly "scientific" anomaly of a fetus developing a benignant Bright's disease, voiding urine containing as high as three per cent. of albumen, and growing fat and sturdy under conditions surely fatal to an adult subjected to a similar drain. In short, the further one searches for the origin and uses of the amniotic fluid the wilder all hypotheses become, unless we accept the simplest explanation—almost invariably the best—that it is secreted by the intra-uterine surfaces for the nourishment of the fetus.

Accepting this, the correspondence of the macrocosmic and microcosmic processes is apparent. The womb represents Cosmic Space—the universal matrix. The fecundated egg focalizes, synthesizes and transmutes or transfers to the material plane the subjective force of the reincarnating entity. From this "point in the circle" exudes not the physical but the spiritual amniotic fluid, the force which causes the physical fluid to flow from the uterine walls, or, in the macrocosm, from Cosmic Space. Following the successive upward steps in the building of its bundle of material sense organs, it is easy to see that each specific process but exemplifies a general law in nature. As has been pointed out, the eye is built up with all its nicety of optical detail and physiological capacity for psychological use without ever having received a single impulse from those light waves to which science would fain teach us it is a specific response. Granite boulders have been subjected to the daily stimulation of direct light waves for untold ages; why are they not studded with eyes? Similarly with hearing. Not only is an exquisitely perfect organ built up in the absence of all but very indistinct sounds, but this organ remains incapable of hearing until certain post-natal processes have taken place.   And so on; not only each sense organ, but also the entire form, is constructed in specific response to an inner directing energy.   It is the return to incarnation of an entity having the spiritual potentialities of sense perception, which become potencies through the opportunity afforded by fecundation and gestation. There is no other rational explanation for the function building the form except as the effect of an inner entity having such function in *potentia*, if not in *actu*.

Thus process after process in embryology might be taken up and the presence of the inner, designing entity proven ; but enough has been pointed out to indicate the train of reasoning which is to be applied to them all, should any desire to carry their investigations further than is possible in this brief and sketchy appendix.

THEOSOPHY.

The Objects of THE THEOSOPHICAL SOCIETY are: FIRST.—To form the nucleus of a Universal Brotherhood of Humanity, without distinction of race, creed, sex, caste or color. SECOND.—To promote then study of Arya and other Eastern literatures, religions andsciences. THIRD.—To investigate unexplained laws of nature and the psychical powers of man.

The following course of reading is recommended to inquirers, viz:

Echoes of the Orient,	$0.50	Esoteric Buddhism, paper,	$0.50
Key to Theosophy,	1.50	" " cloth,	1.25
Seven Principles, Besant,	.35	What is Theosophy?	.35
Re-Incarnation, Besant,	.35	Isis Unveiled, (2 vols.)	7.50
Wilkesbarre Letters,	.10	Secret Doctrine, (2 vols.)	10.50
Letters that Have Helped Me,	.50		

The principal Monthly Magazines devoted to Theosophy are:

THE THEOSOPHIST: "A Magazine of Oriental Philosophy, Literature, Art, and Occultism." Conducted by Colonel OLCOTT, and published at Adyar, Madras, India. Annual Subscription, $5.00.

THE PATH: "A Magazine devoted to the Brotherhood of Humanity, Theosophy in America, and the Study of Occult Science, Philosophy and Aryan Literature." Edited and published in New York by W. Q. JUDGE, (144 Madison Avenue, New York). Annual Subscription, $2.00.

LUCIFER: "A Theosophical Monthly, designed to bring to Light the Hidden Things of Darkness." Founded by H. P. BLAVATSKY. Editor—ANNIE BESANT; Sub-Editor—G. R. S. MEAD; published by the Theosophical Publishing Society, 7 Duke St., Adelphi, W. C. Subscription price, $4.25.

MADAME BLAVATSKY'S WORKS.

THE SECRET DOCTRINE.

The Synthesis of Science, Religion and Philosophy. 2 Vols. Royal Octavo. Cloth. $10.00; Postage, 50 Cents.

THE KEY TO THEOSOPHY.

Second Edition. Cloth. 307 Pages.   Price, $1.50.

www.ingramcontent.com/pod-product-compliance
Lightning Source LLC
Chambersburg PA
CBHW030759020726
47499CB00006B/1687